MW01137227

What the Heck is

Self-Love

Anyway?

What the Heck is

Self-Love

Anyway

?

By Jonathon Aslay

This book is dedicated to

All who strive

For more.

Copyright © 2019 by Jonathon Aslay
All rights reserved. No reproduction of this book, in whole or in part, or in any form
may be made without written permission of the copyright owner.

Front / Back Cover Design by Heather P. Shreve / Copyright ©2019
Credit: back cover photo: David Feder
Credit: profile photo: Starla Fortunato

Table of Contents

Acknowledgments

Like any book project, it is the result of many people and many efforts. I want to thank Jennifer Mathews from the bottom of my heart who, like an angel came down and held my hand and said: *Let's get this book written because it's so needed. "* It would not have been birthed without your talent, generosity, and love. And thanks to Heather P. Shreve, whom I came upon by chance on Facebook. Thank you for taking charge of all the little and big details needed to publish a book. It was much appreciated.

Many thanks go to Jeffery Bernstein, a great and loyal friend whose had my back all these years; especially during the worst nightmare any parent could bear. Your love and generosity is beyond abundant; loving me even when I haven't been very loveable. Thank you for supporting me to get this book written.

Sheri Meyers, a rare friend who became my best friend, thank you for being who you are, the dearest friend anyone could have. I wouldn't be the man I am today if it wasn't for your kindness, care, and LOVE. Thank you for being there through thick and thin.

Katherine Woodward Thomas, from the minute you heard the news of Connor's passing, you supported me with love and encouraged me to get this book out to the world. Your advice has been invaluable, and you've been a loving friend. Big hugs and many thanks go to Joy Kingsborough. You held my hand and heart in support during one of the worst times in my life.

Colin Aslay, from the moment you were born, you lit up and you haven't stopped shinning. As my firstborn, you taught me the true meaning of unconditional love and without that experience, I wouldn't have been able to go deep enough to get this book written. Most fathers love their kids and are proud, and yet with you, there's something more: I Like You. Thank you for just being YOU because you truly are a blessing in my life. I love You.

And Connor "Salty" Aslay—Oh, how I wish you didn't have to leave in order to teach me the most important lesson of all; Self-Love. You have awakened me to so many gifts, especially not taking anything for granted, as well as another important one: don't let anyone f*ck with your chi. Even though your time here was short, you saw we live in a matrix. I'm grateful we shared that mutual belief, and like your big brother, I like you. Just remember, Sacred Circle is always on. I Love You.

Special thanks go to my mother and father, and my brother and sister, to whom I will always be so grateful and all the people along the way who assisted me and believed in this book.

A Note on the Title

If you're like me, you might have tuned out or rejected the idea whenever you hear someone say "you have to love yourself" and you might even say to yourself, *what the heck does that mean?* Unfortunately, loving yourself can be so foreign of a concept and yet it might also be the very thing that changes your life... for the better in every way.

Self-love—our capacity to feed our spirit, fill our 'love cup' and feel inner peace is endless— we just need to tap into it. *But how?* How the heck do we create [or experience] inner happiness?

Well, my friend, it starts with loving yourself. If you're like a lot of people, you might ask: **how the heck do I love myself?**

For some, the term self-love is a turnoff. Instead, it can be seen as self-worth, self-esteem, self-respect, self-confidence, or self-reliance. I'd like to take this idea and expand on that…as far as you can go, as deep as you can go, because love is the universal truth. Everything is constructed and created from the deeper meaning of love; an unconditional love. In this case, of Self.

Many of us go through life expecting outside forces to create our happiness. Whether it's a romantic relationship, more money in the bank, that next promotion, or _____ [you fill in the blank]. There's this subtle, shadow belief—a cultural myth—that somehow happiness resides outside ourselves, just beyond our reach.

That's "when-then' thinking…and it's bullshit.

You don't need a relationship, or a fat bank account, or anything else to experience love and happiness.

All we'll ever need exists within **us**.

So, I invite you to read on… and discover more of what the title—What the Heck is Self-Love Anyway—means. More importantly, what it means **to you.**

Introduction

This book was born and inspired literally weeks after the sudden loss of my 19-year-old son, Connor. My heart was breaking. However, through my loss, I found the courage to write this book because ultimately self-love has the power to heal. Sharing this concept of self-love—in all its forms—has helped me complete the circle, heal, and facilitate the journey for others.

As a relationship and dating coach, I noticed that the absence of self-love magnified any issues people were having. It cemented for me that self-love is the centering factor of your life. The arc of your life depends on it! Just as a keystone supports the stone arch...

...supporting both curves in *the center*.

The Universe blesses us with the experience of learning unconditional love through many types of relationships: friends, lovers, children, pets, spouses, grandparents and so on. Yet, for me, loving myself has been elusive. It's been a real journey to embrace fully (and unconditionally), a love of **self**.

Have you ever flown on a plane and the flight attendant explains safety procedures? If you're like me, you're busy sending out your last text message, or adjusting your seat and not paying attention to the instructions like; "…if there's a sudden change in cabin pressure, oxygen masks will be deployed. Simply pull the string, place the mask over your head, pull down on the string and breathe normally. And if you're traveling with small children, place the mask on yourself first before helping another."

In the years prior to my son's death, I had begun learning how to put the oxygen mask on myself first through various self-help/personal growth books, seminars and inner-child workshops. While the loss of a child is every parent's worst nightmare, I found a place of inner strength and peace in the middle of emotional upheaval and a future without my baby. Love is the vehicle to a deeper level of joy and fulfillment, and the antidote to chaos… which has the power to close the circle when we need it the most.

16

Children are often our best teachers; they remind us and show us that life is much bigger and deeper when you give love freely, are carefree and live life with open expectancy. My oldest son, Colin, keeps that alive in me. The irony is, in order to demonstrate unconditional love to your children, you need to be solid in <u>you</u> and love **yourself** unconditionally. Then the magic can happen!

It's time to put the 'oxygen of love'
on <u>you</u> now.

In the pages ahead, you'll learn a simple approach to inner peace by introducing 30 self-love techniques—ideas and approaches—designed to be read at your own pace. In addition, I'll be turning you onto other books and programs that will change your life for the better.

If you're new to self-help, this will be an introduction (I like to say: a wake-up call) and if you're a veteran to personal growth, this will be a refresher course and a reminder to pay it forward. We all need love and what better way than to gift love (and perhaps this book) to a friend.

With Love,

Jonathon

What the Heck is Self-Love Anyway?

1.

Speak Your Truth; Do It with Kindness

Are you a 'people-pleaser'—afraid to say what you really want, for fear of hurting someone's feelings? As a recovering people-pleaser, I can tell you it sucks. People-pleasers wind up going to places they hate, accepting invitations they kick themselves for, loaning money they can't spare, and generally being doormats. We tell ourselves we're just trying to be 'nice.' No healthy person wants to seem selfish. No good-hearted person wants to be seen as an entitled, self-centered jerk. We all want to be liked. So why does being 'nice' and not saying what we want to, make us feel so trapped?

Because the actions we think of as 'nice' may be our subconscious subtly trying to manipulate others in order to get what we want without admitting it.

Let me say that again:
Nice isn't always nice.

Bad news, right? Here you are trying to be a good human, and I'm calling you a sneaky S-O-B.

Relax, friend. If you find yourself saying 'yes' when you really want to say 'no,' and then feeling frustrated by how it turns out, you belong to a big club.

That club is named *Humanity*.

But here's why learning to speak your truth with kindness ranks near the top of my prescriptions for loving yourself: When I'm not authentic about how I feel (to myself always, and to the other person, when appropriate), my subconscious mind creates an unspoken contract about the great 'sacrifice' I'm making by putting someone else's feelings above my own. And my brain keeps score.

"I'll do it," my subconscious says, "But, boy, will you owe me...big time!" My so-called 'sacrifice' to spare the other person's feelings is neither loving nor free. Instead it's an under-the-table transaction, a pre-planned resentment.

For example, take a date I went on some time ago. Despite my almost instant misgivings after hanging up the phone, I followed through on meeting a woman I'd chatted with online.

"It'll hurt her feelings if I cancel now," I told myself. But before she even got to the restaurant, I was pissed I'd made the offer. The moment she arrived, my frustration shifted. We were a huge mismatch, and I couldn't help mentally critiquing everything from her sour expression to her crappy attitude. Instead of speaking my truth and ending the date, I hung in there, resenting her more with every passing second. She seemed annoyed too, and pretty soon we were practically yelling at each other.

A miserable evening—start to finish. All because I didn't want to hurt her feelings.

So why did I stay? Why not leave as soon as it became obvious we didn't like each other—or even cancel beforehand, as I'd wanted? Why choose to *resent* her, rather than speak my truth? Was sparing her feelings the real reason, or was it something darker?

21

The surface answer is, I was afraid of what she'd think of me. My values dictate that I follow through on my obligations, and I have a professional image to consider. Before my journey toward self-love, I'd have stopped there, grumbled about entitled women, and soldiering on without learning anything.

But self-love means speaking the truth to myself, too.

Over the next few days, with the help of my spiritual mentor, I processed the real lesson of that night. And the deeper story is that I didn't love myself enough to tell my truth with kindness (even to myself), and instead expected a stranger to make me feel good about my character. My decision to go on the date created an unspoken contract for me to follow through and buy dinner because I'm a 'good guy.' The hidden contract required her to appreciate my effort and be a fun companion in return. I was mad at myself for making the bargain in the first place, and when she didn't hold up her end, I resented her too.

On a re-wind, when I had second thoughts, I'd have called her back and given a compassionate but firm retraction of the invitation, something like; "Hi ____, do you mind if I check in with you about the energy I'm picking up between us? Because after we hung up, I realized I sensed a mis-match and need to 'pass' on our date..."

My mentor suggested practicing using the words aloud, getting used to saying what I really mean.

It's uncomfortable. But it gets better.

The Universe gives us 'do-overs,' and not long after that miserable date I had the chance to speak my truth with kindness on a phone call with someone with whom I'd texted several times. Her demeanor and tone told me right away we weren't aligned, and I was able to say what I felt while staying kind. She confirmed the mismatch and we ended the conversation like two healthy grown-ups.

Learning to speak my truth with kindness has eliminated a ton of pre-planned resentments and freed me to be more present and loving when I do say 'yes.'

2.

Stop F*#%ing Complaining!

This self-love story is short but powerful.

Stop. Freaking. Complaining.

I've heard a hundred variations of this conversation at bars, in airports, even on coaching calls: "I'm just letting off a little steam" or "Life isn't fair, and I've got the bruises to prove it."

All my friends agree. When I complain about my job, my partner, or my finances, they nod and chime in with their own stuff. It feels better knowing I'm not the only one with problems." If everyone does it, how bad could it be? What's the harm in complaining?

It's <u>literally</u> making your life **worse!**

<u>Complaining vs. Venting</u>: Complaining is noticing what is wrong **without taking responsibility for the situation** and without deciding what you can do to change it. It's laying blame, giving away your power, immersing yourself in negative thoughts and telling yourself you're helpless.

Healthy venting is recognizing and taking responsibility for something you don't like; whether it's an emotion you need to work through, a situation that's causing you distress, a relationship you're unsure about.

Venting is empowered problem-solving. Complaining is asking someone to affirm our victimhood.

Let's be honest—problems are real. Pain hurts. People disappoint us, leave, get sick. We have genuine grief to get through, financial difficulties to overcome. But complaining is a life-sapping, poisonous soup we cook up and share with our friends, hoping the act of sharing makes us feel better.

Studies have shown that each time we complain, we make victimhood easier and taking positive action harder. Complaining literally rewires our brain, shortening the electrical pathway between noticing something we don't like and the sense that we're helpless. The nerves grow closer together with each repetition, until complaining becomes our first and easiest neurologic response. Add in the stress hormone, cortisol, which spikes whenever we're feeling threatened, and our physical body gets hit with screwed-up sugar metabolism, hormonal disturbances, and sleep disorders—all from complaining.

Even worse, because we're wired for empathy, when we hang around other people who complain, our brains respond as if we're the ones doing the bitching!

One of the most powerful acts of self-love is to stop poisoning yourself with negativity, now.

Stop. Effing. Complaining.

So, what's the alternative, and how do we change? The alternative is *taking responsibility*, which we'll go into more in later lessons. But let's reiterate here that complaining is completely different from healthy venting. Healthy venting is admitting I'm responsible and willing to deal with whatever is causing me pain, no matter the cause. When I need to vent, I ask myself whether I want advice, perspective, or merely a friend to stand present while I work out my own solution. Sometimes I journal about the problem. Then I check with my friend to see whether he's up for helping me work through the issue. When we're finished, I thank him for his time and attention, and remember to be a healthy friend when it's his turn to vent.

How do you stop complaining? *Simple.*
Stop. Freaking. Complaining.

I said simple, not **easy!** But you can begin right now:

THE THREE A's TO END COMPLAINING:

Awareness: I'm unhappy with XYZ situation.

Acceptance: I'm responsible for dealing with XYZ situation.

Action: The action I'm taking is_____. (or NO action)

Go 24 hours without complaining. Try it. See how you feel. Your brain (and body) will thank you.

3.

You're Human.
Mistakes <u>Happen.</u>
{Even When You're Doing Your Best}

How do you feel when you screw something up? Embarrassed? Guilty? Ashamed? What happens if your screw-up becomes known? Do you publicly excoriate yourself, or get angry and look for someone else to blame? Do you secretly believe that if you beat yourself up for your mistakes, you'll bully yourself out of making them altogether?

So, let me ask—
how is that working so far?

In your life, have you ever met *anyone* who's perfect? I haven't. And those who claim perfection usually turn out to be ordinary, flawed humans with secrets that don't stay hidden.

There is a better way… and that's to unconditionally *love yourself* when *you make mistakes*.

This process can dredge up some serious resistance. When I suggest adopting a new way of looking at errors as something to be embraced, what feelings come up? If you're like me—and almost everyone I've coached—the concept of admitting we'll never stop making mistakes triggers a deep, paralyzing fear: The fear of *Not Being Enough.*

Am I *enough?*

In our journey toward self-love, we need to evolve past the ego-constructed beliefs that keep us stuck. One particularly damaging belief is the idea that we have to be better than we actually ARE in order to be lovable.

Right here, right now, we need to acknowledge the reality that, like it or not, you and I are imperfect humans. We're going to make mistakes, no matter how hard we try. We can't change reality. But we can change our FEELING about that reality. And we can change the story about what that reality says about us.

I would simply ask you, are they <u>really</u> mistakes if they propel us forward? Where you are **now,** in the context of your journey, is perfect.

How do we flip the script so we can love ourselves unconditionally when we make mistakes?

We can begin by recognizing that we're responding from ego adaptations (by getting angry at ourselves for our foul-ups) instead of from a deep sense of self-acceptance and love (knowing we're lovable, mistakes and all).

To move toward self-love, try this trick:

Imagine yourself as a child—maybe as a four-year-old—figuring out the world by observing, evaluating, and adapting. If you have friends with kids that age, think about that four-year-old's reasoning ability. It's pretty limited, right?

Now see yourself as that little kid, then see yourself making a mistake. Note how you feel inside your chest, and what fear comes up.

Here's what a client shared recently: "One day in kindergarten someone gave us packets of Boston Baked Beans candy—weird little red things with spikes on the outside. On the way home from the bus, I popped one into my mouth, crunched, and found out I hated the taste. I spit it out and tossed the rest onto the grass. When I got home, my mom was disappointed. Turns out, she loved the darned things. That was almost fifty years ago, and I can still recall how bad I felt knowing I'd let her down."

Any kid would try to figure out a way to keep from disappointing mom in the future. But how could she know her mom liked something she'd never seen before? This is why the beliefs we formed about making mistakes need to be examined and reshaped.

It probably won't surprise you that this memory came up during a discussion about my client's relationship with her partner, and the insecurity she feels when she makes a mistake. Loving ourselves when we make mistakes is important work.

Our old beliefs color

our current relationships, whether we realize it or not.

So, go back now and imagine yourself as that four-year-old, feeling bad about a mistake. View the situation from your current state as a wise, experienced adult. Everything looks different, doesn't it? Does the big, scary mistake you made render 'little-kid-you' any less lovable? Of course not!

Now sit down and tell your younger self what you didn't understand then—that what seemed like an unforgivable error was simply the kind of flub everyone makes. You may even want to give that kid a hug so he or she knows it's okay. Even if you're skeptical, try it! You may be surprised at how well it works.

Picturing yourself as a little kid (or if that's too hard, imagining another child that age that we care about) teaches us to *have compassion for ourselves* despite our mistakes.

Learn to be compassionate... towards YOU.

Learning compassion for ourselves when we make blunders opens the door to all sorts of wonderful new experiences:

o   We stop beating ourselves up for errors, real or perceived.

o   Paradoxically, as our fear subsides, learning gets easier. We lean into the lesson offered by the 'mistake' and find ourselves responding better without trying so hard.

o   We become humble and less judgmental. We stop comparing, feel more 'a part of' rather than 'apart from' other people.

o   We see ourselves (and others) as lovable no matter where we are in this journey of life.

Ultimately, if we persist, we begin to welcome mistakes as opportunities for growth, personal insight, and the chance to become a more conscious, loving human—both toward ourselves and toward others.

You're human. Mistakes are inevitable. But self-love flips the story we tell about our humanity, transforming those mistakes into gifts!

4.

If Something Feels Off, It Is! {Trust Your Intuition}

Have you ever had a strange feeling, ignored it, and later wished you'd listened to your gut?

Our culture has trained us to ignore our inner voice. To push through, try harder, bulldoze our way to our desired goals. We want something, and we go after it. Yes, there's value in persistence but many of us blot out our innate wisdom to pursue something our ego tells us we <u>need.</u>

We hear the wise inner voice—
then tell it to shut up!

In contrast, self-love teaches us to inquire deeply, listen to the song of our inner voice, and seek the highest potential for our lives. Intuition is the beacon guiding us through the rocks.

When I'm coaching clients after a relationship ends, what they often tell me is they knew something was off right away… but wanted to give the person the benefit of the doubt. As we work through our experience, we may even find out the problem had nothing to do with the other person, and was instead a deep, subconscious issue they'd never faced in themselves.

Does that mean their intuition was wrong? NO!

Your intuition is ALWAYS worth listening to, no matter what.

Even if you're not sure what the voice means— ESPECIALLY if you're not sure what the voice means—give yourself time to listen. Honing your intuition is a skill that deserves practice. Whether it's an internal issue or a problem with the situation itself, our intuition lets us know we're moving in the right direction.

A client shared an experience the other day that shows the value of intuition. She'd made a connection with a man from a dating site. They talked on the phone and agreed to meet later the next week. Instead of calling again, he went back to using email, which sent up a red flag for her. He'd seemed nice, and they had a lot in common, but as the date got closer, she began to feel heaviness in her chest she described as dread.

The dread got worse, and a few days before the date, she sent him an email (his chosen method of communication) telling him she was nervous about meeting and perhaps wasn't ready after all. She was apologetic but honest.

He never answered.

My client says it's the best gift she's ever received. Her intuition had told her to pause. She listened, even while admitting the problem might be hers rather than with him. His reaction confirmed the mismatch, and his inability to respond with a 'sorry it didn't work, but good luck' revealed that her intuition had been a wise guide.

The next man she met was a great fit—loving and gentle and understanding. Nine months later they became engaged.

How do we hone our intuition? How do we discern between normal nerves and a warning from the wise inner voice?

Listen with loving curiosity.

The next time your inner voice gives you a nudge, instead of ignoring it (or buying the first explanation that comes to mind), pause, and ask what it wants you to know. If you find yourself saying, "Yes, but…" you may be bulldozing your way toward an outcome rather than letting your intuition be your guide.

Exercise: When you sense your intuition is trying to tell you something:

o   Identify the sensation in your body (heaviness in chest, queasy stomach, throat tightening).

o   Breathe into the sensation without judging or hiding. If you can, be compassionate toward the feeling.

o   Ask what you're afraid to admit, even to yourself. You don't have to change course if you don't want to, but you owe it to yourself to be honest.

o   Write down your fear/worry/doubt. If you need to, use code.

o   If you could respond any way you like without negative consequences, what would you do?

o   Now, imagine you've taken the action. How do you feel inside? Relieved? Disappointed?

There may be some false starts, but over time you'll learn to trust your inner voice. Besides, as we'll learn next, when we're living a life based on love, there are <u>no mistakes</u>—just opportunities to grow!

5.

Don't Let Anyone F*ck with Your Chi

Have you ever had your day ruined by a total stranger 'going off' on you in the grocery store? An irate customer throwing personal insults at you for someone else's mistake? A passing driver shooting you the finger because you had to slow down for traffic?

How long did it bother you? A minute? An hour? A whole day?

How much of your life energy do you waste because of someone's mistaken opinion about you? If you can relate, this is a great chance to practice self-love: Don't let anyone f*ck with your Chi.

This lesson came from my beautiful son, who passed away from an sudden accident a month after his nineteenth birthday. My heart still aches as I write this, but I wanted to share the gift I received as Connor's dad, watching and learning from this wondrous young man.

Even as a child, Connor had Ninja-level skills at letting the opinions of others roll off his shoulders. If a teacher or family member would get upset, he'd pause a second, then shrug it off and continue with whatever he thought was best. At first it was maddening. As I grew more conscious in my own life, I began observing him with curiosity, then with admiration. How could a kid his age be so unbothered by other people's negative opinions?

One day I asked him, and he said, "Dad, if someone has a problem with me, that's THEIR problem, not mine."

Boom.

My teenaged kid, who had no formal training at building inner peace through self-love, somehow innately knew *not to take anything personally*—an idea Don Miguel Ruiz refers to as the Second Agreement in his short-but-powerful book, *The Four Agreements.*

The metaphor goes like this: Each of us stars in a movie in our heads, based on thousands of beliefs about ourselves and the world around us. We filter everything though the lens of this movie. Unfortunately, our lens never matches perfectly with anyone else's. Nor is it the absolute truth. It's our UNDERSTANDING of the truth, as viewed from inside our movie.

Not taking anything personally is really freaking *hard*, because when someone hurts our feelings, we feel actual pain inside our bodies. We tell ourselves THEY hurt us. If they have a negative opinion of us, we feel sad, ashamed, or betrayed, and the physical sensation in our chest makes it seem like they've actually harmed us.

Finding inner peace amid this 'not-good-enough' feeling is tough.

Kind, authentic feedback is entirely different from someone's opinion. We talked about giving kind, authentic feedback in the section on speaking your truth, and we'll discuss receiving honest criticism later. Instead, we're working here on letting go of other's OPINIONS that don't apply to you.

If you're confused, let's get perspective using an example that may be silly but instructive.

What if, in someone's movie, there's a character named Brett? Now, let's say your name is Julie. You, Julie, are confident in your name and identity. You know who you are, and you know beyond a shadow of a doubt that you are not Brett, no matter what anyone says. But this person really, REALLY needs a character named Brett, so they walk up and call you Brett. How do you respond?

Here's where it gets interesting, and where I learned so much from watching my son. Connor knew who he was, and he knew he had a choice of how to respond to unfair or misguided opinions from others. Because he was a loving, secure kid, he would consider their words for a moment, then essentially say, "Huh. Looks like you're looking for someone named Brett. That's not me, but good luck."

He knew not to take the other person's mistaken opinion as having anything to do with him. He didn't take it personally. And, most importantly, Connor was compassionate. He KNEW he wasn't Brett, so he didn't feel the need to defend or deny or be angry. If someone called for Brett, Connor simply didn't answer. Does that make sense?

Everyone has an internal 'movie' that filters how they experience life. When someone incorrectly assigns you a role in their movie, you don't have to be angry or defensive. In fact, feeling defensive may be a signal you're secretly wondering whether you ARE Brett, and that's a great chance to find out whether you really love yourself for being who you are!

So, no matter what,
don't let anyone f*ck with your Chi.

6.

Be of Service
to Humanity

A few years ago, I learned a valuable lesson about service. When I set the intention to serve humanity without expectations, my life exploded in new and beautiful directions. Before every coaching call, before every meeting with a client or colleague, before writing a new post or recording a Facebook Live, I'd take a moment and ask the Universe to help me be of service. Suddenly, instead of planning what I'd say, I found myself listening deeply and sharing authentically. Being present in the moment, I became a better mentor, colleague, father, and friend. Service is now a way of life rather than something I do a few times a year.

At this point, let's clarify what I mean when I talk about service to humanity. To me, service is quiet, compassionate action that recognizes we all need each other. There's no pity or one-upmanship. We're all equals, and at some point, we all need the love and support of our fellow humans.

"A clear sense of purpose
made every day an adventure."

So, it's important to check your motive. Is the act ego-feeding (coming from a place of emptiness) or truly generous? Most of us have done both, but when I serve with a sincere desire to help others, peer-to-peer, expecting nothing, I'm always blown away by joy and gratitude in the moment. It's an old adage, but true—it really IS better to give than to receive.

So how does it work? How does being of service to humanity generate self-love?

To me, it's about attracting more of what I give out. When I serve others (especially from a sense of gratitude and abundance,) I notice all the love, abundance, and goodness in the world, and I feel better about my life. When I love my life, self-love flows naturally.

We'll talk more later about the laws of attraction, but here's one way to think about it. Have you ever researched a car before deciding what to buy? If so, you probably found a make and model you liked, maybe even took one for a test drive. Then, if you're like me, while you were shopping for your dream car, you started noticing the same model on your street, on the highway, and in parking lots. A week ago, you didn't give that car a second thought. Now you're seeing dozens. They're everywhere!

Being of service works the same way. Where we direct our time and energy towards something, it tells our mind what to notice. Share love, and you see love everywhere. Give without expectation, you notice when you've received unconditional love from other people. Strive to be part of something larger than yourself, you begin to see humanity connected in an amazing tapestry of love. It's like magic.

What about self-care and filling our own cup?

Here's why it's critical to distinguish between ego-feeding, and those acts of service that come from a place of gratitude and abundance. By the way, ego-feeding doesn't necessarily mean grandiosity. Feeling lonely (unlovable) makes us fearful, and unless we're conscious, we can operate out of external ego instead of love. Then it's easy to unconsciously slip into 'rescuer mode' and look for someone to help, hoping they'll thank us and make us feel worthwhile. We give more than we're able, and we feel like martyrs— resentful, put-upon, starved for the same attention they're giving out. They give more than they are able, hoping someone will notice. Having done my share of this, I can tell you it's miserable.

As I said earlier, motive is everything.

One trick to discovering our real motive is to ask whether we'd be helping **if no one ever found out.** So, before I volunteer for any service commitment, I check in with myself on whether I'm coming from a place of giving without any expectation. Sometimes the answer is 'no,' and I'm forced to look inward to see where I haven't taken good care of filling my own cup. If the answer is 'maybe,' I ask whether I can serve without any shred of resentment. If the answer is 'yes,' I give with gusto.

Service to humanity is one of those paradoxical principles where we receive far more than we give. It's an incredible experience; both a source and result of self-love. Try it and let me know what you find. Let's go make the world a more loving place!

7.

Take Responsibility for Your Choices

This is a radical idea, because taking 100% responsibility for one's own choices means NEVER playing the role of victim, no matter how unfair life seems.

It's easy to blame outside forces for things we don't like about our lives.

Getting mad at our jobs, lovers, finances, traffic, or taxes seems completely justified. While blame is a normal development stage for children, many of us reach adulthood still looking for scapegoats. Some never grow out of it.

Even if we 'wake up' and recognize patterns and the role we play in our lives, we sometimes stop there. "Sure, we messed up," we tell ourselves. "But did you see what THEY did?"

Deep down, we secretly believe...we'd be happier if other people, institutions, and circumstances would behave the way we wish.

Maturity requires new thoughts and new actions. If we want inner peace, we need to grow up.

Because the truth is, even when we're hit by random circumstance—say, a car crash or the death of someone we love—**we still own the power of choice in how we respond.** The event may be out of our hands. But the response is 100% ours, <u>always.</u>

So how do we evolve from seeing ourselves as victims to taking absolute responsibility for our choices?

There are fantastic online resources for learning how to recognize our unconscious tendency to play the victim. If you're unfamiliar with the concept, The Karpman Drama Triangle is a great starting place. (See Resources in the back.)

For me, the key to owning my choices has been to show up with curiosity, kindness, and compassion; to ask whether (or more accurately, HOW) I've subconsciously put myself in the situation and if so, what inner conflict I must be trying to work out. If the situation is truly beyond my control, I ask how learning from the experience can transform me into to a more loving, present, authentic person.

This is really personal for me. When my son Connor died, I was thrust into a waking nightmare no parent ever wants to experience. There was (still is) no way to think about my son's death as anything but a tragedy. My heart was (still is) broken into a million pieces. How could I not feel like a victim in a world that would take away my beautiful son?

In the midst of the most crushing, unendurable pain I've ever felt, a thought washed over me:

*"I have a choice in how to face this. I can be a victim—and everyone will understand and feel sorry for me—or I can choose **Love.** The pain will still be there; some days I won't be able to breathe for the weight of it, but maybe—just maybe—there's something to learn in all this."*

Like any grieving parent, I wanted to crawl under my covers and never come out. It didn't feel fair. Still doesn't. All of us feel like victims sometimes. But it's a dead end.

Nothing will bring my son back (every cell in my body cries out when I write that. Sometimes I have to just stop and let the tears come) but his loss has crystalized my priorities, eliminated all trivial, ego-driven distractions, and taught me to be absolutely, completely, *radically* present with my other son.

Self-love meant seeking the gifts in a parent's worst nightmare. Those gifts were only possible through the power of taking responsibility for my choices.

8.

Everything Happens FOR You, Not to You

Are you a victim or a victor? YOU decide…

This concept throws a lot of people, because bad things do happen—or so they seem at the moment. But think about the people you admire who possess amazing courage, wisdom, and character. Did they get that way without going through hard times? No!

Fire hardens steel.

In your life (and mine), the worst things we experience reveal reserves of inner strength we never knew existed. In

53

black moments, it's hard to look for the light. But choosing to approach life as a victim keeps us from seeing how we can use experiences as a springboard to growth.

Feeling unlucky, put down, or picked on is a signal we've unconsciously slipped into victim mode. So, right here, right now, I challenge you:

DECIDE …
to see all problems as opportunities.

Besides, how do you know things won't turn out better than you imagine? There's an old proverb that goes something like this:

In the village lived a wise old man who owned a magnificent stallion. One day the stallion ran away, and the man's neighbor said, "Oh, what bad luck you've lost your horse."

"Good luck, bad luck. Who knows?" said the wise man.

The next day the horse returned with a beautiful red mare. The neighbor said, "What great luck, now you have the beginning of a fine herd!"

And the man replied, "Good luck, bad luck. Who knows?"

The man's son decided to train the mare. Being wild, she threw him and broke his leg. The neighbor shook his head sadly. "What terrible luck that your son's leg is broken."

The old man said, "Good luck, bad luck. Who knows?"

Soon after, the Army came through the village. All young, able-bodied men were required to go to war in a far-off land. Because his leg was broken, the man's son was spared. He grew strong again, married, and had many daughters and sons who loved hearing their grandfather's stories. They passed this story to their children, and to their children's children, as it is now passed to you...

When something occurs (the job is lost, the relationship is over, the accident happens), judging the experience as 'bad' forces us into feeling like a victim. Instead, decide to think about the experience—whether you initially see it as good, bad, or neutral—as a hands-on lesson in this amazing laboratory we call Life. It's not easy to retrain the brain. But consciously looking for positives embedded in every experience opens incredible new channels for growth and problem-solving.

Victims stay stuck. Victors forge new paths.

It works the same with worry about the future. My clients sometimes share that they're afraid of getting hurt in relationships, envisioning doomsday scenarios about someone they haven't even met. When we change the focus to how much they learned from past experiences, how glad they are to be out of relationships that didn't work, they relax and envision new possibilities. Life gets fun!

Self-love means realizing that everything can happen FOR you, or it can happen TO you. The choice is yours. If you feel like a victim—and we all do sometimes, so don't beat yourself up—you can shift your thinking and become a student in this laboratory of human experience. When you see all things as a growth opportunity, you'll look back and realize you've gained strength, courage, and wisdom. You'll become less a victim of life and more often a victor.

And being a victor is a hell of a lot more fun!

9.

If It's Sincere {and From the Heart} You Can't Say the Wrong Thing

Self-love is being our authentic selves in all situations. When we speak from a place of sincerity and compassion, authenticity becomes our gatekeeper, helping us identify people who are aligned with us and easily release the rest. The idea of authenticity in all situations dredges up a lot of fear for my coaching clients, so let's explore why it's safer to be authentic than to create a false mask of pleasantry.

Take a scenario where you've met someone you're interested in. On the first date, you find yourself attracted at multiple levels. You're having fun! Then they say something that raises a question about a critical value like monogamy. While they haven't come out and said they date multiple people, you're listening for clues and still can't tell. Then he/she asks whether you'd like a second date.

Now you're faced with a choice: A) Keep silent, go on the next date, and hope you're wrong about him/her being a 'poly romancer,' or B) Speak up—sincerely and authentically—and find out. When we work on this, my clients say: "But I don't want to seem pushy/needy/bitchy and ask probing questions on the first date." *Really?*

You care more about what he thinks than your own well-being? That's the opposite of self-love! And it's not good for anyone.

Here's why not choosing authenticity sucks. First—and I've seen this hundreds of times—let's say you go out on more dates, trying to be fun and flirty without asking hard questions. With each date you're taking a chance of becoming more attracted to someone who doesn't share your values. Once the heart gets involved, it's hard to let go. *Ironically, being authentic actually protects your heart.* Second, and this is important, if you aren't honest about who you are and what you value, the other person doesn't have a chance to know you either. This is where fear of rejection comes in. (If they see me, will they like me?) It's also why real intimacy starts with self-love.

You have to know...

... you're lovable already.

If we surround ourselves with people who don't really know us, we don't feel safe. Conversely, when we share our deepest selves, we give others the chance to support us as we truly are—warts and all.

So, imagine sharing your truth on that first date, saying something like, "Hey, I want to let you know that when it comes to romance, I only see one guy/girl at a time. How about you?" Whether the person gets mad, dodges the question, or gives a straight answer, you'll learn more in 30 seconds than you would have in hours of trying to catch hints.

Even if you fumble the delivery, someone who shows up authentically themselves will applaud your effort and match it. If they don't, you'll avoid expending time and energy with someone where the relationship doesn't stand a chance.

Notice I didn't say **wasting** *time and energy.*

This is the final piece of why if it's sincere and from the heart, you can't say the wrong thing to the right person. When you're authentic, no matter what happens, you'll LEARN from every situation. You might decide to screen people better before agreeing to go on a date, or you may learn it's not as scary as you think to be authentic from the get-go. You might simply get to practice having compassion for someone who hasn't gotten very far in their own journey of self-love.

If you're happy with how you showed up, you'll congratulate yourself for your honesty. If you'd like to have done it differently, you'll calmly assess what happened and make whatever changes seem right. Either way...

...there are no mistakes. Only lessons.

Ironic, isn't it? Having no self-regard, which is another way of saying you don't love yourself, means you'll assign that job to someone else; in this case a virtual stranger. When we practice self-love by being authentic, we're constantly growing, constantly learning, showing up as our true selves and becoming freer. We're letting go of ego and reaching for deeper understanding. When we're authentic, we're paying attention to ourselves and everyone else. We're students in this classroom called Life, tapped into the force that connects us all. I believe that force is **love.**

And in love, there are no mistakes.

10.

Your Body is a Machine, Not A Temple

I'm sure we've heard the phrase, "Your body is a temple, treat it as such." In other words, there's this air of mystique around it; as if you need to treat it pristinely to reach some unattainable perfection. So, I ask—*really?* My philosophy is more scientific; your body is a machine—albeit an amazing one—which responds to environment, food and exercise. Give it what it needs, and you will be richly rewarded!

Adopting a healthier lifestyle will always benefit you because it benefits the machine. The good news is, the body is malleable, forgiving, and forever trying to heal, if you give it the right stuff. But it doesn't have to be an *absolute* or a strict way of living. For some, it is a strict way of living, and for others, they've found a happy medium that works for them. No one lifestyle or health plan works for all, but there is something comforting in the fact that, if you figure out what works for you, you can live a rich and rewarding life indefinitely.

Find a routine that works for you and adapt it to fit the changes that life brings.

Life is also a machine of pleasure and so adopting a bit of pleasure is equally as important as adopting a strict regiment of treating it as a temple, if you will.

Intrinsically, as you practice self-love, it will become easier and easier to treat your body with love. In essence, treating yourself WELL. As you become at ease with your journey and more passionate about your future, you will naturally put health at the top of your priority list.

This is one of those investments in **you** that really pays off.

Health is a gift.
It's all in the way you unwrap it.

Think of your working on your body in baby steps. If you're struggling with your weight, then do it in baby steps. If you're already in good shape, then keep doing it in baby steps. And if you're in fantastic shape–if you're treating your body like a machine, great! You don't need this chapter.

Micro steps create macro results.

Sure, we all have those health hiccups—we get sick, injured, broken, dinged, and laid-up. There's always the unforeseen bump in the road. However, if your machine is in tip-top shape, you will be able to take those 'speed bumps' more gracefully.

Think of your body like a car. How are you going to treat it over its lifetime? Are you going to get regular oil changes? Wash and wax it, make it look its best and protect the paint? Or are you going to neglect even the basics and run it out till it dies?

Accept where you are and then check-in with yourself to see if you are, in fact, taking the best care of <u>you</u> that you can. For me, the idea of a temple was too large an idea. Looking at it like a machine made it a little easier to comprehend, digest and wrap my brain around.

I've adopted a regiment of walking each day for my heart and recently took a deep-dive into the facts about preservatives in food and food that has been altered. By foregoing processed foods, and eating whole foods for my fuel, I have lost 20 lbs., sleep better and my blood pressure has dropped.

So, create and write three modest health goals to start. The more specific you are, the more chance for success. Write down the time of day and the duration, and why you're doing them. It can even be time set aside to do research about health on the internet so you are informed.

And, let's face it! If you aren't 'fueling' the machine on a regular basis, how are you going to take care of, love, cherish and enjoy the people around you? There's no time like the present to treat our bodies the best we can, which—by definition—is one of the highest forms of self-love. When you feel well and energetic, the sky is the limit! And isn't that the essence of self-love?

Love is limitless… so let it also power your machine and see what happens.

11.

The Importance of Community, Develop a Tribe

Hillary Clinton once said, "It takes a village," and a lot of people mocked her, but I believe that community is hugely important for a level of inner-peace. Having your circle, your tribe, brings an ancient practice into being. The desire to have community around us stems from our DNA. Scientifically and biologically, we needed a tribe to survive in the 'old' days. We were—and still are—social animals.

The Ancients knew the wisdom of a tribe...and all its benefits.

Your tribe can be family, co-workers, friends, or a mix of all three. Don't have a tribe? *Then make one!* Go to a church function, join a Meet-up, go network, or start a Meet-up! But start going places to create and cultivate friendships with *people.*

And, even though modernity has taken the immediate physical need away for a tribe on some levels, we still need one <u>emotionally.</u> *And* we still need people in general to interact with, have babies with, work with, etc. [I can assure you that twenty years of the Internet Age has not wiped out millions of years of evolution!]

Which leads me to qualify and define the word.

When I say 'tribe'—I mean an in-the-flesh tribe, not some internet group on Facebook. Not a <u>virtual</u> connection. I mean face to face! Virtual connections present an emotional 'trap' for some who believe they are creating **real** connections. They are not!

Because social media encourages promiscuous 'friending' —creating tenuous connections at best—people sometime stop nurturing their REAL friends altogether. I call this a 'faux' connection or friends. When the sh*t hits the fan, are these virtual friends willing to BE there? Most likely, no.

In the U.S. today, nearly 1 in 4 Americans say they have no one they could turn to for support. Modern Western communities have become unmoored from traditions and extended social groups. The resulting 'individualism' may be at the root of one of the greatest modern stressors: *lacking a strong sense of shared purpose.*

I'm thinking of the TV show "Golden Girls." Four women in mid-life who choose to live together—a group of friends dedicated to each other for **life**. We know now that smoking, obesity, happiness and even loneliness all have been shown to be contagious. So, it stands to reason that the longest-lived people are in communities where most people are making healthy choices—yes—but more importantly, there's emotional security. They know that someone is always there for them.

Tribes, to some degree, still give us protection...at least from being alone.

When you don't feel alone, you feel closer to humanity and closer to an inner-peace. And you'd be surprised how quickly a tribe can grow! We have a fundamental need to bounce ideas off one another, ask questions, get opinions, advice, love, support, comfort and the list goes on and on. Tribes makes us BETTER. When we're together, we become each other's mirrors, from which we can reflect and be reflected. We grow and learn at an accelerated pace; much faster than if we only had ourselves.

In truth, it's vital that we commune. Because, still today, it **does** take a village.

I'm afraid we're stuck
with each other…
and what wonderful glue we are!

12.

Your Thoughts Create Your Feelings

If you're like me, and the people I coach, emotion causes a physical sensation. When I'm sad, my chest feels heavy. Sometimes my throat tightens—like there's a lump inside—and I cry. When I'm joyful, my body feels light, buoyant. Laughter bubbles up spontaneously.

With that in mind, notice what you feel inside your body. What emotion do you associate with that feeling? After you've identified the feeling, take a few breaths, empty your thoughts, and let it all go.

Now do this: Think about the last time you felt wild, unbridled joy. Where were you? Who were you with? Remember the weather, the smells, the sensations. How did your body feel in that moment of pure exuberance? Were you encased in a golden warmth? Did you walk on air?

Really feel it in your body; the incredible physical sense of joy.

Now come back to the present, breathe, and check in again with the sensations in your body in this moment. What are you feeling now? Is your body lighter than when we started? Is your breath easier and deeper? Notice whether you feel even the tiniest bit better.

If you're like me, the test above shows that you can choose, at least for a few seconds, what you think about. And it also proves that *what you think about directly affects your feelings.* Amazing, right?

Let's apply this to the bigger picture.

Today you'll generate thousands of thoughts. Some will be jobs on your to-do list, some will be a recap of your conversations. Some thoughts will be about the past as viewed through your memory, others will be about the future as viewed through your hopes and fears. A lot of those thoughts will affect your feelings. If you're mad at how your boss spoke to you, your shoulders could get tight. You're angry. If you suddenly remember that her kid is in the hospital, you might—literally—shrug off her rudeness and wish her well. How you think about the conversation will influence your feelings.

Therefore, consciously or not, your thoughts create your feelings.

Outside factors may start our minds down a path. But where the mental thread leads us **is a choice.** And, as we discovered above, where your thoughts travel, your feelings follow.

Where thoughts go, feeling flows.

Here's why this matters: Since you picked up this book, you've already recognized how important it is to *behave lovingly* toward yourself. Self-love means understanding that when I think of myself as a victim, I end up feeling small, weak, and less-than. The thoughts I choose directly affect my emotions.

This became painfully obvious to me in 2009, when the market crash left me financially devastated. I've recovered now, but at the time, aside from figuring out how to live on nothing, my biggest challenge was to remind myself daily that my income had no bearing on my value as a person.

To be honest, I felt like a failure. It took hard work to reframe my thoughts and view the setback as a chance for me to reorder my life according to my values of personal growth and service to humanity. Today I see the crash of 2009 as a huge gift.

The wound is the place where the Light enters you. ~Rumi

In the months after the crash, I faced reality and drastically cut my lifestyle. Then I looked for something—anything—to be thankful for every day. No matter how bleak life appeared, I always found it.

Soon, despite the worst financial downturn of my life, my feelings shifted from shame to inner peace. Gratitude replaced fear. New, inner confidence replaced my old reliance on outside approval. My mission changed to helping others find their own path toward loving their own true self. All because I experienced a personal failure and decided to think about it differently.

That's self-love.

13.

Heal Your Childhood Wounds

Do you have any recurring patterns in your life—a succession of romantic relationships that go nowhere? Money challenges that never resolve? Jobs that seem great at first then end up eating your life? Do you start a new diet every year? Join a gym and never go?

If those aren't your patterns, try looking at your list of New Year's resolutions. Were any of them on last year's list? How about the year before that...or TEN years before that?

There are good patterns, too. Maybe you're always early to appointments and keep your car spotless. Maybe you're the go-to person at your office for getting projects done, or the one everyone counts on to bring dessert to the party.

This isn't about assigning guilt, it's about getting real.

Remember how I promised tough love? Well, this is it! Whether we realize it or not, we all have patterns. You, me, everyone. Behaviors we repeat, day in and day out, usually without conscious thought. Patterns are a fact of life. Some help you thrive. Others keep you stuck.

Once you're open to recognizing your patterns, you'll realize your whole LIFE is built on repetitive behaviors, both healthy and unhealthy. How do we change those that hurt us?

The key is to find the BELIEF behind the behavior.

Change the belief and the behavior will follow. Let me say that again: Until I looked for the beliefs that caused my unhealthy behaviors, change was impossible. But when I went deeper and looked for the WHY below my patterns, I was able to release those that hurt me and others.

So where did those beliefs originate? In childhood!

If you don't believe me, the next time you're upset, check in with yourself and notice how old you feel. If you're angry—I mean really livid—think back to the FIRST time you felt that way. How old were you? What was happening?

Most importantly: what rule did you invent to try to make sense of the circumstance?

If you're like me, you'll find dozens, maybe hundreds, of those kinds of 'rules' embedded in your subconscious. Some, like being prompt, I've kept because I'm happy with the results.

But the belief that everyone needs to like me (whether or not I like them) has kicked my ass my whole adult life.

Some rules are exact opposites of others, so no matter which rule I follow, I feel guilty. How screwed up is that?

So, how do we uncover all the rules from our childhood and release those that sabotage our wellbeing—what some refer to as childhood wounds? There are some really good methods out there. I chose one called The Hoffman Process. The Process helps you become conscious of (and disconnected from) negative thought patterns and behaviors on an emotional, intellectual, physical, and spiritual level. Through this process I slowly removed habitual ways of thinking and behaving and began to align with my authentic self.

Besides finding compassion for the little kid inside me who did the best he could, uncovering and healing my childhood wounds has had a surprise bonus: I'm rarely offended anymore. If someone goes on a tirade at me, I don't get angry or turn into a doormat. Instead, I see the wounded child in them and decide how to respond, whether by removing myself from the situation or asking what's really going on with them. Sometimes I need to apologize and make amends, but more often, they've broken some unconscious childhood rule and are mad at themselves more than me.

14.

Choose Love Over Ego {Fear}

This seems like an easy choice. Of *course* we choose love, we tell ourselves. We're good people. Jerks have big egos, and we're not jerks. But the truth is that all humans deal with ego. Psychologists tell us it's a normal phase of development, of learning to recognize ourselves as individuals.

Maybe it is normal, but my view is that ego is a block to love, an adaptation (or maladaptation) we've developed to cope with our fears. Ego will always be with us, and sometimes is even rewarded with material success. Yet, we all have seen or heard of ego-driven people who appear successful on the outside but never find inner peace. There's a long, sad list of celebrities who've ended their lives despite having everything but inner peace. To me, it's because comparison, measuring up, and ego all create separation. When I come from a place where I win/you lose, I'm operating out of fear. In that scenario, my happiness depends on external conditions instead of self-love.

Self-love lets me know I'm okay no matter what happens on the outside. My ego is no longer in charge of keeping me safe.

So how do we choose love over ego?

First, recognize that when something f*cks with your inner peace, you're probably stuck in ego and fear. You're never going to completely dismantle fear, but it doesn't have to be in charge. You can **learn** how to switch to love.

When someone makes you feel triggered, angry, or indignant—especially if you're still having a mental conversation with that person hours later—there's a good chance your ego is driving the train. Ego tells us we're right and the other guy is wrong. The magic happens when you stop arguing your position and get curious, both about your own fears and those of the other person.

Would you rather die on the hill of 'Right'- or have good relationships? And life?

You can always stop and ask yourself, "What am I afraid will happen? What does it say about me if I do/don't do this thing?" If you're paying attention, your ego will reveal your biggest fears. And really, what do you have to lose except a deep sense of unhappiness?

As a dating coach, I've seen clients overlook potential healthy partners because of ego-based ideas about wealth, appearance, and professional choices. One of my clients recently shared that, because of ego, she'd always been attracted to men with advanced degrees. She's a doctor and worried she wouldn't have much in common with someone with less formal education. After a hard marriage and divorce from another doctor, in a relationship based on competition and looking good for the neighbors, she was ready for a new way of life.

We worked together on uncovering her fears, including her distorted beliefs about self-love and the need to prove her worth with outward appearances. She realized she'd been shoring up her own insecurities (fears) by choosing a partner who looked good on paper, while disregarding those qualities she truly wanted like kindness, humor, integrity, emotional maturity, and intellectual curiosity.

A short time later she met a man who makes his living with his hands. Because of our work, she was able to set aside her ego and become curious about his inner qualities, and in so doing, discovered a healthy, loving, growth-oriented life partner. Instead of superficial appearances, they're focused on helping each other become the best versions of themselves, inside and out.

Ironic, isn't it, that her ego had driven her to make choices that made her LESS HAPPY? By giving in to her fears about her worth and financial security, she'd chosen a marriage that made her feel less worthwhile yet financially secure. Self-love gave her the inner security to attract a partner capable of giving and receiving love.

Ego and fear never bring inner peace.

Love does, every time. If you take home one message reading this book, I hope it's this: **Choose love!**

15.

There is No Separation Between the Genders

This may sound controversial, so bear with me.

First, let me clarify that I realize there are differences between genders. Obviously, there are people with penises and people with vaginas—and people with variations of both. This chapter isn't about how we identify, reproduce, or about the polarity of sexual attraction.

This is about how we treat each other.

Respect, kindness, compassion, and love aren't exclusive to either sex. When we segregate and treat people differently because of their sex, we annihilate our chance for unconditional love.

Ideas about gender roles, chivalry, dominance, submissiveness, masculine energy, and feminine energy (especially if we're pressured to conform) invite comparisons. Comparisons lead to a sense of 'otherness,' and seeing someone as 'other' leads to separation, which destroys love.

We're all human, period.

And we're a lot more capable of self-love when we shed embedded ideas about our respective genders and just focus on being good to each other. Don't' believe me? Okay, let's try this scenario:

We've all been taught that protectiveness is innately masculine, and that receiving is primarily a feminine trait. But what about the woman who stops her friend from stepping in front of a car? What about the grieving man who seeks a hug from a loved one? Aren't they simply people showing the positive qualities of protectiveness and receiving love?

All humans possess a measure of every quality in various combinations.

When we reject any of our characteristics,
we're turning our backs on
important parts of ourselves.

In turn, we judge other people for having those same qualities. Sometimes we envy or longing; other times we feel angry.

You can't love yourself if you hate some of your parts.

Why limit yourself? Become the best whole human you can, embrace all your qualities, regardless of their historical association with one sex or the other. Celebrate your completeness and love every bit of yourself, not just those parts our culture assigns to your gender.

You're a whole human, valuable **just as you are.**

So is everyone else.

In my practice as a dating coach, when a client complains about a man not taking the lead in the relationship, I ask why she is handing over her power. This usually surprises her, because most of the time she has no idea she's giving away her sovereignty. Once we get clear on what she wants, I coach her on being authentic and speaking her truth. If her partner is emotionally mature, the conversation brings them closer. If not, she has a new sense of her right to create the life she loves, whether with a partner or not.

Ironically, I'll sometimes see clients struggle with entitlement, and when we dive deeper, we discover her underlying fear of not feeling equal to men has created a sense that she needs to get even. Separation between the sexes fosters game playing and one-upmanship. But when we see each other as interconnected humans, all with equal value, we stop assuming motives, excusing bad behavior, and setting aside our own values to keep relationships afloat. We'll stop giving away our power, evaluate our desire to connect with each person based on their abilities, and make decisions for our own wellbeing.

Letting go of separation between the sexes is an important step on the journey toward self-love. I hope you'll fearlessly examine your own biases—and their underlying beliefs—so you can begin to see yourself and everyone else as valuable and whole, as equal and connected members of the human family.

Learn to love ALL your qualities, masculine and feminine and those in-between. You're worth it!

16.

Understand and Accept Others' Experiences

The next self-love concept is learning to accept and maybe even appreciate people who seem ugly on the inside.

If you're like me, you've spent hours, days, maybe weeks off balance because of someone else's actions. Humans can be real assholes, and getting over a genuine wrong is tough, especially when we didn't do anything to deserve the action.

But being off balance hurts us, too.

So, it's an act of self-love to find our way back to inner peace.

How do we do that?

The way I see it, when it comes to dealing with people who have done us harm, we have two choices: We can hold onto the energy of being hurt and destroy our inner peace, hoping our resentment will somehow protect us. Or we can restore our integrity—*our wholeness*—by trying to understand and accept the other person's experience.

What about people who've hurt us or done terrible things? What about really, REALLY bad people, like Hitler?

Okay, let's do an exercise on Hitler. What was his motivation for invading Europe and for committing genocide? He wanted power. Why did he want power? To feel in control. Why did he need to be in control? Because, internally, he felt *out of control.* What kind of person feels out of control? A child who's been abused, abandoned, or parented without appropriate boundaries. What happens to a child in those circumstances? They grow up without a deep, internal sense of self-love and need to create havoc outside themselves to compensate. Sometimes that havoc has tragic, global consequence. There are no excuses for Hitler's actions, period. But...

...acceptance isn't the same as approval.

Let me say that again, because it's a big block for a lot of us on reaching a place of acceptance:

Understanding someone and accepting their experience doesn't mean absolving them of responsibility for their actions.

This isn't a suggestion to forgive and forget, or pretend it wasn't that bad. That's denial.

Hitler murdered millions. Regardless of his childhood wounds, he was responsible. The same goes for those who commit crimes, lie, cheat, or behave badly in relationships. Even something as minor as ghosting in the dating realm can be traced back to that person's internal lack of self-love.

The question is how WE deal with other people's bad behavior. Because, while their action is 100% their responsibility, our reaction is 100% our responsibility. And being off-balance, triggered, fearful, rageful, and victimized robs us of our personal power to respond in the best way for ourselves and everyone else.

Can you hear what I'm saying? Our best response always comes from a place of inner peace. And when we're harmed, understanding and accepting others' experience is the path back to inner peace. Seeing the offending person as a wounded child is a good way to start the journey. Some of my friends use The Prayer of St. Francis as a meditative guide.

As we've talked about before, when we're hurt, we need time to feel and process our feelings. But holding on to rage only makes us less effective. Holding on to fear makes it harder for us to make good decisions for ourselves. Holding on to the belief that some people are bad for no reason only fosters despair and a sense of helplessness. We're locked in a perpetual state of Fight, Flight, or Freeze—none of which allow us to create positive change in our own circumstance.

Decide to make your inner peace a priority, regardless of who or what has harmed you.

Understanding others' experiences and finding acceptance—even when we strongly condemn the actions—is a way to restore our balance, inner power, and ability to respond.

And that, my friends, is self-love!

17.

Make Personal Growth a Daily Habit

Self-love isn't a destination. It's a dynamic process, forever shifting according to your intent.

Merriam-Webster defines the word <u>dynamic</u> as "*marked by usually continuous and productive activity or change*," which means that when I achieve a moment of inner peace, I <u>can't</u> check the box marked self-love, congratulate myself, and kick back in my recliner for the rest of my life. Alcohol recovery groups remind members:

There's no such thing as coasting uphill.

Personal growth operates on the same principle. If you're not growing and getting better, you're heading the opposite way.

Think of self-love as a muscle that needs consistent work to stay strong. Or like a daily shower to clean off life's emotional funk. You brush your teeth every morning, even though you just brushed them the night before. Even on a good day, stuff builds up.

Besides, life keeps happening. New issues emerge. Kids grow up, our parents age, WE age.

Yesterday's tools may not solve today's problems.

That's why I suggest making a daily habit of improving your internal environment, whether that's starting each day with a meditation, reading from a favorite text, or listening to an audiobook. One of my favorite books for starting the self-love journey is THE UNTETHERED SOUL, by Michael A. Singer. Many of my clients appreciate A RETURN TO LOVE, by Marianne Williamson. Others prefer religious texts or recovery books. Whether it's a book on the Twelve Steps or Don Miguel Ruiz's excellent book, THE FOUR AGREEMENTS, look for literature that feeds your soul. If you search with a pure heart, you'll find a wealth of online tools, classes, and workshops. I am a graduate and strong supporter of in-depth programs like the Hoffman Process.

In my own journey of self-love, I've developed a morning routine that includes listening to at least fifteen minutes of new information from an audiobook, podcast, or TED Talk, usually during my morning walk by the beach near my house. Some people keep a journal about what they discover as they learn. I usually share my perceptions with one of my growth-oriented friends or study groups I belong to.

Fifteen minutes a day can change your life!

"But I don't have time," you say. "My schedule is already packed so that the idea of adding one more task makes my eyes water." I hear you, I really do. But this takes less time than standing in line at Starbucks for a latte. Less time than clicking one headline in your newsfeed. Ancient people were busy too, often with actual life-and-death issues. But consider this ancient Zen proverb:

"You should sit in meditation for twenty minutes a day, unless you are too busy. Then you should sit for an hour."

The seventh of Stephen Covey's *7 Habits of Highly Effective People* is Sharpen the Saw. If you've ever tried cutting down a tree with a dull blade, you know it gets harder with each stroke, until eventually you're using all your strength with ZERO reward except blisters and sore muscles.

If you wake up one morning and realize you aren't making headway in your life, check in on whether you're investing daily time in personal growth. Chances are, you've placed other priorities ahead of your internal development.

When will you begin that long journey into yourself? ~ Rumi

That's okay. We all have times where life encroaches. Don't beat yourself up. But decide right now to resume your work, knowing that doing so makes you a better friend, partner, co-worker, and all-around human.

Making personal growth a daily habit is a small thing, really. Fifteen minutes a day. But this small commitment can literally alter the course of your entire life. Aren't you worth fifteen minutes of your own time?

I say you are!

18.

Pay Attention to the Signs

In the months before writing the outline for this book, my life got really chaotic. My dating coach business had morphed into teaching clients about self-love, which meant creating tons of new support material. My personal life had taken a turn which I was still processing. Then, within a short period, I lost both my mom and my son. My dad, who's in his nineties, now needed care that fell to me. To say my priorities shifted would be a gigantic understatement.

But I kept on the path of inner exploration, took care of myself, and did all the things suggested in this book. I connected with people I love, cried when I needed to, and slowly began to heal.

Several weeks in, congratulating myself on handling my grief, I decided not to reschedule a seminar I'd committed to give on Conscious Dating. This is in my wheelhouse and talking to people gives me hope.

The morning of the seminar, same as every other morning, I rode my bike along the beach trail, thinking about all the wisdom I'd impart that evening. There's a construction zone on the trail, heavy gravel and loose rocks, with a sign that advises getting off and walking your bike. But I was in a hurry and wanted to get back home. Besides, I'd survived a rough few months, and the sign was just a suggestion. So instead of dismounting as I had every other day, I kept one foot on the pedal and pushed along with my other foot, like you would a scooter.

What happened next is painfully predictable—almost as painful as my bruised ribs and badly scraped wrist and forearm.

A few hours after my bike wreck, every breath was agony, and I was forced to take a mild pain pill. That night, my well-planned talk about conscious dating turned into a fun-but-rambling group chat about radical self-care while dating.

Feedback from the attendees was great, but I was disappointed in myself for not delivering the experience I'd intended.

In a conscious life there are no mistakes, only learning opportunities.

As my ribs healed in the following weeks, the lesson was clear: Pay Attention to the Signs.

Even when you're busy—*especially* when you're busy—take a moment to BE IN THE MOMENT. Or, as my friends in the Twelve Step programs sometimes say, "Keep your head in the same time zone as your ass."

Paying attention to the signs also means listening to your body. If you're like me, you've had times when you told yourself you were too swamped to take time off and then found yourself stuck in bed with the flu, forced to rest against your will. Our bodies tell us what they need, and if we ignore them too long, they'll mutiny.

Parking tickets, fender benders, skipped appointments, medical issues that turn into emergencies, missed deadlines—all can be signs we're spending time somewhere other than RIGHT NOW. So how does one get in the moment?

It's easy. Take four deep, relaxed breaths, inhaling slowly

through your nose and exhaling through your mouth. Let your belly rise with each breath, feel it fall. Relax your shoulders and jaw as you breathe, slowly, easily.

Now, sense your feet inside your shoes. Where are your feet? Feel them touching the ground. What do you feel under your legs? Thighs? Seat? How does the cloth feel against your skin? Notice how your breath warms your upper lip, how good the air feels going in and out of your lungs…

Where are you right now? Here and now? If so, that's good. If you need a few more breaths to really center, go through the cycle a few more times, paying special attention to relaxing your upper body; your neck, shoulders, and arms.

Now that you're here right now, what signs are asking for your attention? Is it something from outside, a suggestion or literal sign (like *walk your bike*) that will make life smoother if you listen? Or is it a sign from inside—a twinge that tells you to make that doctor or dentist appointment you've put off. Do you have an urge to call a friend you haven't seen in a while? To tell your mom, dad, sibling, or your kiddo that you love them? If you hear a small voice inside telling you to do these things….

… listen.
Pay attention to the signs.
You'll be glad you did.

19.

Fall MORE in Love with Nature

Self-love is all about caring for our own wellbeing; providing ourselves the love we need to become our highest-functioning, most effective selves in this lifetime. What better way to show love than to feed yourself sunshine, fresh air, and beautiful scenery! So, let me ask—do you have a favorite nature spot? If so, how often do you visit? Monthly? Weekly? Daily?

Mine is the ocean. Some years ago, I made living at the beach a priority. Now, as part of my self-love practice, I spend time near the ocean every day. Here's why you should find

your favorite natural habitat and make it part of your daily
routine:

o It's a chance to reconnect to the source of life.
Humans are built from the raw materials of the natural
world—oxygen, carbon, hydrogen, minerals.
Watching the waves roll in during my bike ride every
morning, I feel renewed, regenerated. Nature feeds
me, gives me energy to do whatever is next in this
adventure.

o It's a reminder that life goes on. When my brain wants
to obsess over some event or circumstance I can't
control, nature offers a glimpse of eternity and helps
me gain perspective. The sun sets over the Pacific
Ocean every day, as it has every day since the oceans
were formed. Sunsets paint the sky on good days and
bad days alike, unaffected by our human joys or
sorrows. However important my issue seems at the
moment, there's always a larger view, a deeper
perspective that will help me regain my inner peace.
Connecting with Nature opens the door to this new,
larger perception. All I have to do is step through.

o It's humbling. Can you stop the leaves from turning gold in the Fall? Are you able to influence the tide or change the direction of the wind? The most powerful person in the world is helpless to alter nature, and to me that's pretty damned comforting. Nature is the great equalizer. When my ego gets too inflated, it's a reminder that I'm just another inhabitant on this big blue sphere. When I'm feeling less-than, I think about how lucky I am to witness all this beauty. I'm instantly right-sized.

o Your inner child likes to play, and Earth is a big, wonderful playground. Think about all the cool things you noticed in the schoolyard as a kid, even if you grew up in the city. You might have seen a weird bug crawling along the sidewalk, clumps of clover growing out of cracks in the concrete, crows fighting over a scrap in the parking lot. Maybe the bug had one of those iridescent shells, maybe there were tiny yellow flowers in the clover—miniature versions of a buttercup, and maybe the crows sounded like your family having an argument. You may not live near the ocean or have easy access to a park or local forest, but Nature is everywhere if you remember to look. Give your inner child the joy of discovering some aspect of the natural world to appreciate every day.

o It engages all the senses. So much of our modern life is limited to audio/visual tasks that we tend to neglect the rest. One of my favorite parts of my morning ride is feeling the ocean air sting my face, tasting and smelling the salt-tang on the back of my tongue. Most mornings I pause at the halfway point and sit on the dune for a few minutes, sifting my fingers through the cool sand. On the days I'm not able to ride, I find myself less conscious of touch, smell, taste, and my life is slightly less rich. Humans are sentient creatures, which literally means we sense our surroundings. Nature invites me to use all my senses and love what they show me. How cool is that?

Give yourself a gift of five minutes of contemplation in awe of everything you see around you. Go outside and turn your attention to the many miracles around you. This five-minute-a-day regimen of appreciation and gratitude will help you to focus your life in awe. ~ Wayne Dyer

You may be convinced there isn't enough time to get outside, but if you make the commitment, you'll notice small things that help you connect with our Earth. Whether you live in the city or suburbs, near mountains or desert, when you seek out Nature, you'll fall in love. And that's a form of self-love!

20.

Love Being Alone

How do you feel when there's no one else around? Content? Anxious? Lonely? Do you turn on the television to drown out the silence? Compulsively check social media to see whether anyone liked your last post? Call someone you haven't talked to in a while?

If you think you're great alone, do me a favor and check in with yourself the next time you're on your own for the evening, when it's just you in an empty house with your innermost thoughts, fears, and insecurities. No distractions, no white noise. Just you and hours of silence. Be honest...

How do you feel when you're really, *really* alone?

If you're like most people (including me before I began this journey toward self-love), the quiet is deafening. We'll do damned near anything to avoid facing the idea that no one else is thinking about us at that moment; that we're really, completely, totally on our own. Solo. A single, microscopic speck wandering a universe so large we can't conceive of its boundaries.

Terrifying, right?

One of my clients says it's like being pushed off a cliff. Another describes it as floating in the space between planets with no lifeline. Faced with those perceptions any rational person would grab for human connection, a distraction, a Facebook mention—anything to keep from feeling as though you've been set adrift without an anchor. But learning to love being alone is vital to the practice of healthy self-love.

So, if you don't truly, completely love being alone, I'm going to ask you to do something hard:

Just let go. Really.

The next time you're by yourself for a time, get comfortable—some people prefer lying down—then breathe slowly, close your eyes and float. Listen to the internal presence that speaks love with a still, small voice. If worried thoughts crowd your mind, picture the frightened child inside you and say these words:

I love you.

I'm sorry.

Please forgive me.

Thank you.

Repeat them as often as you need to until you feel calm inside, then keep going. Be alone with yourself inside your skin, breathing, listening, *being*. Usually it doesn't take long to come to a state of inner peace, a place of pure, golden calm. Stay there for a bit longer and something really amazing may happen—instead of feeling alone, you'll feel intimately connected to EVERYTHING.

Most people who practice loving being alone reach a state of knowing, deeply and surely, that they are safe and loved no matter what is going on in their individual lives or in the world at large. They have a sense of the infinite, of the never-ending time and space and energy of All That Is. Their fear (and ego) subsides, and the love they feel for their true selves extends to every other living being in the form of compassion.

This isn't the Pollyanna-like delusion that everyone is wonderful if you just love them enough, but a deep, grounded wisdom that allows you freedom to care without losing your center. It's finding your own power and stepping into a place of autonomy so you can make good decisions about how you want to show up in relationships.

Because, ultimately, we have to reach peace in our solitude in order to become healthy friends, partners, or lovers.

In relationships, we'll come up against our fears. Loving being alone allows us to face and heal those fears (which sometimes means changing or ending the relationship) rather than staying stuck in a bad relationship because we're afraid of being by ourselves…or alone.

The most important relationship you'll ever have is with yourself. Isn't it worth learning how to love being alone with your lifelong best friend…? You!

21.

Love the Space You're In

How do you feel when you're in life's limbo? Maybe your company is talking about downsizing and you don't know whether your job is safe. Or, your last romantic relationship ended a year ago and you still haven't met anyone compatible enough to get past a second or third date. Maybe you're taking care of an elderly mother who should move into assisted living, and you're dreading that call that announces she's taken a bad fall.

Maybe there are no impending changes at all, and you are looking at your life wondering whether you're caught in a rut?

You're a person who likes action, and right now you're stuck waiting.

Waiting…

W.A.I.T.I.N.G.

(Deep sigh.)

If you're like me, you need forward motion, and a pause feels like wasted time.

But what if the waiting is a gift?

What if it's a powerful stop—

the sweet silence between movements

in a brilliant piece of music?

In a life built on self-love, nothing is wasted. Not even waiting.

So how do we learn to 'love the pause'?

The key is to become fully present. Understand this: whatever is happening right now, at this very moment, is you interacting with the Universe in a way designed for your maximum benefit. Becoming very still and inhabiting your body, breathing into what IS in this moment, you'll find something of value—some lesson, some insight, some increased capacity for humility, compassion, or resilience.

One of my clients described the awareness this way:

A year into a horribly contentious divorce, after numerous court appearances, unsuccessful mediations, and tens of thousands in lawyer bills with no end in sight, she felt completely stuck. Nothing worked to move the proceeding forward. She couldn't buy a house, move, or even commit to a new schedule at her job until things were settled regarding custody of the children and division of assets.

One morning she went for a run on her favorite mountain trail. Despite her overwhelming worry, she decided to list all the things she was grateful for—loyal friends, her spiritual mentor, a lawyer with a conscience, a legal system that afforded at least some protection, a roof over her head, healthy children, the ability to earn money. The longer she ran, the longer her list became. She savored the strength in her limbs, the warm air in her lungs, the earth-scent of the trees.

Then it hit.

If the divorce had been easy, she would never have learned how strong she was.

Many generations of women in her family had stayed with men who mistreated them. She'd been taught from birth to be submissive, to accommodate the needs of others over her own. In fact, part of the reason she'd stayed so long in a bad marriage was the fear of not being able to generate a good life for herself and her children.

But here she was, fighting for her and her kids' well-being and doing a damn good job of it!

Suddenly it became clear that the pattern she'd been in wasn't a dead-end purgatory after all, but a lesson very specifically designed to help her become a stronger, healthier, better version of herself. An easy divorce may have been a nicer experience, but she wouldn't have learned what she needed to, and may have ended up with someone worse.

She was overwhelmed with the 'rightness' of waiting, even though it was hard. Now, years later, she still gets emotional telling the story. Looking back, that awareness was a turning point in her life, as she is now financially self-sufficient and in a happy and healthy relationship based on mutual respect. Most importantly, she respects herself, which wouldn't have happened without that long, dreadful three-year period where absolutely nothing got resolved.

So, the next time you're stuck waiting, ask yourself...

What lesson are you and the Universe co-creating for your <u>own</u> benefit?

Get really quiet and find gratitude for what IS, even if you're not happy about everything. You'll find magic in the pause. I promise.

And if you persist, you'll learn to love the space you're in.

22.

Make Friends with the Voices in Your Head

Can we get real for a minute, I mean really cut through the crap and talk plainly about why I wrote this book?

I wrote it because I would love the world to
Wake the f*ck UP!*

(*Actually, I want all of us to wake up, to become fully aware of the effect our thoughts, feelings, and actions have on ourselves, each other, and the world.)

Many of us, including me before I started this journey, waste years wandering through life with blinders on, focused on meaningless, ego-driven goals, measuring life's worth by the size of our bank accounts or the cost of our cars. We aren't intentionally shallow. We're simply listening to the voices in our heads—the product of cultural and family conditioning—and doing what they tell us, never questioning, never wondering whether our actions will really bring us peace.

We are unconscious.

If we want to wake up, we have to learn to notice (without judgment) what our internal voices are telling us, then decide whether to act on their advice.

What voices, you say?

In his excellent book, THE UNTETHERED SOUL, Michael Singer teaches how to identify the internal voices we all hear, to notice what they tell us without judging or reacting. This, he says, is the beginning of true freedom. An awakening to our genuine selves. The beginning of consciousness.

Take a moment now and listen to your inner dialogue. Sit quietly for 15 seconds and notice your thoughts. Just observe without trying to change or alter them. Can you hear a skeptic complaining that this chapter is too far-fetched? A worried admission that you've always suspected there were too many people in your head, especially when they all talk at once? An uncomfortable whisper that maybe you're missing some ingredient happy people seem to possess?

Our mind generates constant chatter, always driving us to want more. Listening to those voices, we're sure we'll be happy once we achieve the next thing, whatever that happens to be—bigger, better, prettier, faster, thinner, richer.

<u>Satisfaction</u>, our minds tell us, is *over there*...

Problem is, when we reach that milestone, there's always another. Our minds are change engines, always seeking, never satisfied. That's the nature of unconscious living. It's our ancient survival mode, mis-applied to modern life.

It's the reason some people never learn inner peace.

And the voices don't stop there. Acting as judge and jury, they're a constant source of criticism, directing a low-level insect hum of disapproval toward us and everyone around us. *I should've remembered that guy's name...should have turned left back there... should have paid that bill last week. For crying out loud, why is that idiot driving so slow in the left lane? Why doesn't my kid/spouse/co-worker pay better attention? Don't they see how hard I work? Can't they hurry up and finish this road construction?*

Once you've identified the chatter, pay attention to how often it's wrong. Sometimes my inner voice gives me crazy, conflicting advice. "Call her—no, don't! She'll think you're an idiot. Wait, maybe she really did mean it when she said she looked forward to our next date…"

If we want genuine, deep peace that springs from self-love, we have to learn to separate out the internal critic and release ourselves from needing to act according to its instruction. And we have to go one step further—to learn how to listen to that voice with compassion, recognizing that it often comes from a part of our psyche that is wounded and afraid. Someone who is afraid needs love and reassurance, not condemnation.

We need to make friends with the voices— and not let them run our lives.

That's the magic of THE UNTETHERED SOUL. When we apply the tools Michael Singer teaches, we learn to calmly listen to the restless, anxious voices, recognize what parts of ourselves they represent, and then use our highest, most wise selves to decide how we will respond. We come from a more mature emotional place and make decisions based on love and compassion rather than unconscious, fearful reactivity. We act from a place of love for ourselves, for others, and for the whole world.

And that's what this book is all about!

23.

Be a Good Steward of Your Money

Talking about money in a self-love book may seem odd, so bear with me. Let me expand on how self-love overlaps becoming a good steward of your finances.

Our ego-centered culture reveres money as a symbol of power and worth. Taken this way, especially if you're trying to move away from shallow motives, money can seem like a dirty necessity, an ugly fact of modern life. Maybe you're uncomfortable with the idea of having money or wanting to generate more than you currently do. But what if we define money differently?

What if ... money is really just an extension of *energy?*

Think about it. All of us acquire money by expending some sort of energy—whether by physical exertion, creative effort, intellectual work, or simply trading our time and attention for a paycheck.

My mother was a good steward of her money and therefore energy. She used money, not as a tool for manipulation, as so many people do, but as a way forward; a way to demonstrate love. Personally, I prefer to view money as an extension of energy as it correlates to *expending personal energy.* So, as we continue, if you find yourself equating money with greed—stop and ask which definition you're using.

Now that we've reframed money in terms of personal energy, let's talk about how to take good care of it. Here's where the self-care comes in. Think about what you value most in life. Do you cherish friends and relationships? Travel and interesting experiences? Having a home to entertain in? Helping others?

Great! Now make a list. Don't worry about what anyone else thinks. If shoes make you happy, so be it. But ask yourself how long you felt happy when you bought your last pair. If you can't remember, that should tell you something.

This is your energy, your life, your list.

How important is financial security to your sense of wellbeing? How would it feel to have six months' worth of expenses in a savings account? A year? What about freedom? How would it feel to live near the beach or take a break from your job and volunteer in a place you've always wanted to visit?

Give yourself permission to imagine a life that feels amazing and worthwhile.

Now that you have a clear list of your values, let me ask a simple question—are you directing your personal energy (money) to the highest priorities on your list first?

When I first looked at where I was directing my energy, I had to admit my money didn't match my priorities. I wanted to live at the beach and devote more time to deepening my relationships and helping people. Instead, I was spending all my money on an expensive place I didn't like, with a closet full of crap I didn't wear and a car that drank gas like crazy.

Instead of being a good steward of my personal energy, I was using it to acquire STUFF. Then I learned to think about money as personal energy and to care about how I used it.

Now, I pay myself <u>first.</u>
My priorities, my list, my life.

Now my home has a view of the ocean, one that is smaller, which means I need less furniture to make it comfortable when friends visit. Because staying healthy is a priority, I ditched my sports car for an economy model, and I ride my bike for local errands. My life revolves around relationships instead of accumulating things, so I'm able to work in a field I love with an income that meets my needs. Instead of more stuff and clothes [that I can't possibly use], I invest in personal growth and saving for a rainy day.

Since money no longer symbolizes worth, my ego is out of the way. Every day I'm free to use my personal energy— my money—in a way that best reflects my personal priorities.

Seeing money as personal energy reordered my thinking in other ways, too. I used to expend a lot of time and energy making money, but never felt satisfied. Now I direct my personal energy toward creating lasting, authentic, deep relationships, and I have inner peace. I used to exhaust myself at work and tell myself I was an important guy. Now I experience each moment as it occurs, each breath bringing fresh sensations and understanding. I live in the present, where my personal energy connects to the limitless universe and all that **is.**

It's a vastly different way of living, with incredible benefits for me and for those I care about. That's why self-love means being a good steward of your money. Your personal energy is yours alone to manage.

Love yourself enough to take good care of it!

24.

Don't Love Others at the Expense of Self

What does **love** mean to you? Is it clean dishes, a love poem, a diamond ring, or filled-up gas tank? Is it sending someone warm thoughts and a handwritten card? Or is love holding their hair when they vomit after chemotherapy?

Is love a feeling, an action, or both?

Think about how you'd describe loving someone. Most of us come up with words like sacrifice, selflessness, compassion. We're taught that love means surrendering your wants and needs to serve the people who are important to you.

Some take it to the extreme, believing that if it hurts, it proves you care.

Most of us have, at times, given our loved ones more time, money, or emotional energy than we can afford. We tell ourselves we're doing it for **love**, and maybe that's true. But does depleting ourselves to the point of collapse really help anyone? And can we still call it love when we wind up physically or emotionally spent, resentful at those we say we care about?

This journey of self-love offers a better way. And that's to *avoid loving others at the expense of self.* But isn't that selfish?

NO! An empty well leaves everyone thirsty.

So, don't run yourself dry trying to love someone. Instead, love from a place of strength, replenishing your internal stores when you run low. The natural world provides great examples of this, from a wolf caring for her pups to birds encouraging nestlings to fly. Even historical religious figures, revered for their incredible sacrifices to humanity, took time away from the crowds to sleep, eat, and fill their own spiritual cups. It's a rhythm as natural as life itself. Love flows for a time, then the giver rests.

That's great, you say, but how can we achieve the right balance of loving others without neglecting ourselves?

It starts with this critical fact:

> *Keeping your well full is*
> *100% your responsibility.*

Let me say that again.

You are ONE HUNDRED PERCENT in charge of making sure you get enough rest, emotional support, and time for yourself to replenish your stores. You are ONE HUNDRED PERCENT responsible for knowing how much financial and physical reserves you can offer someone you care about, and for making sure you don't overdo.

In other words,
create healthy boundaries.

The reason I started with self-responsibility is because there's this myth that if we love someone enough, they'll love us in return, and we'll be filled up. And that's complete bull. That's giving to get—the exact opposite of unconditional love.

Problem is, 'giving to get' never works. Even when someone genuinely loves us, they can't possibly know what our deepest needs are, and if they do, they can't possible do for us what we're not willing to do for ourselves.

Giving to get inevitably makes us feel hurt, misunderstood, resentful. When we're resentful, we unconsciously slip into manipulating with guilt or complaints, hoping the person we love will meet our needs, feeling abandoned when they can't. It's a miserable cycle that leaves everyone feeling awful.

Loving from a place of strength is entirely different.

When we accept responsibility for meeting our own needs, our love pours out from a deep well of true, unselfish desire to show we care. We don't expect (or need) any particular reward, and we're okay if things turn out differently than we imagine.

Loving this way is an amazing, freeing experience! Love begins to feel like an unlimited, benevolent force, an infinite energy you tap into and direct rather than something that's generated from inside. It's hard to explain, but when you pay attention to your own human needs, you'll become a conduit for love. And your job then is to keep the conduit strong and viable.

Here's what this looks like in a practical sense:

In my own life, before I show up for someone in a loving way, I check in with myself on what I'm able to do and stay healthy. My father recently needed a lot of help, and part of my decision about my role in his care included being honest with myself about how much time I could offer every day. Taking care of an elderly parent sometimes left me nostalgic and sad, so I had to become super intentional about making sure my schedule included fun, too. Rest, fun, time to recharge…all part of the daily care plan I made to help him through his health issue.

I love my dad. Before beginning this journey of self-love, I may have done more than I should, and resented him for it. Giving Dad my time and attention from a place of strength made a tough situation better. The same has proven true with friends, colleagues, family, and romantic partners. Loving more than you're able is a trap that leads to resentment and pain.

So as much as you're tempted, don't love others at the expense of self!

25.

Get Out of Your Head and Feel Your Feelings

This probably sounds counterintuitive after my suggestion that your thoughts create your feelings, so let me explain.

Whether we realize it or not, feelings have energy of their own. Like demanding toddlers, emotions refuse to be mashed down, ignored, or hidden—at least for long. If you don't give your feelings space to exist, I promise they will screw with your head in ways you can't predict. They can come out sideways as anger or sadness or resentment, hijack your relationships, sabotage your goals, even attach themselves to someone else in the form of projection.

127

One of the most loving things we can do for ourselves is learn healthy ways to feel our emotions. It's how grown-ups learn to behave like adults.

But our society teaches us to be afraid of feelings. Even those fortunate to have good parenting are pelted with messages that we "shouldn't feel" certain emotions. Don't feel envy when your friend gets a new car. Don't be disappointed if you didn't get Christmas gift you wanted. Don't feel sad when your life changes, when your marriage ends.

Suck it up. Get out there. Have a drink.

Don't feel.

Then, when we're happy or proud of ourselves, people warn us not to get too high or we'll have farther to fall. They say we'll get a big head, that we're fooling ourselves if we think life is always this easy. So, we deny our feelings. Hide them. Turn ourselves into pretzels trying to avoid them.

We get numb.

There may be gender differences, but in my coaching, I've seen both men and women having trouble accepting and feeling their full range of emotions. Anger is okay for some, but not sadness. Others are good with happiness and run like crazy from disappointment.

Why do we need all those feelings, anyway? We've already said that our thoughts influence our emotions. Why not just cast aside bad feelings or talk ourselves out of them?

The reason is honestly beautiful: Because we're
human.

Feelings give us love, connection, empathy, courage, bonding, joy, longing, attraction, hope. Feelings make us ache to hold our new baby, pump our fists when we land the dream job, cringe when we see a puppy being abused. Good feelings make life amazing. Even so-called negative feelings show us things about ourselves and our relationships that lead to our inner growth.

But squashing our emotions is the opposite of self-love. It's *telling ourselves that how we are at that moment isn't okay*. The trick to not intellectualize our feelings and not take them as facts. Let me say that again:

Feelings need room to exist.
But feelings AREN'T facts.

We need to learn how to process emotions without letting our thoughts gallop a million miles in the wrong direction. It's not easy, and it takes practice.

Here's what I tell my coaching clients about giving emotions room to exist without letting them take over. It works for them, and it's what I use. When an emotion hits, instead of mashing it down, try to really be present and let the feeling come in like a wave. Think of yourself on a beach in ankle deep water, and your feeling is a wave washing over your feet.

Don't go deeper into the story about WHY you're having the emotion. Just let it approach and break over, knowing it will eventually recede. Don't run away. Be curious.

Notice how you feel, but
don't <u>do</u> anything.

Let me say that again, because it's important:

This isn't the time for thinking, making decisions, or taking action. Your thoughts *can* change your emotions, but you don't want that right now. All you're doing is giving your feelings calm attention without judgement, maybe for the first time in your life.

It's important to stay ankle deep, too. Remember the wave? It will tug at your feet for a moment then leave, same as your feeling. If you feel overwhelmed, stop. You can always come back later. The purpose is to love yourself, so be gentle. I've found it's easier to feel my feelings than to deal with all the junk that goes with pretending they don't exist.

Let's take anger, for example.

What if the next time you're pissed, instead of telling yourself to "get over it," you give yourself permission to really tune into that anger in your body? Hopefully you'll find somewhere you can let go, shut the door, and give your anger your undivided attention. Maybe you'll stomp around the house, swear and growl. Or maybe you'll just sit and feel. Most of all you'll keep breathing, noticing, paying attention. If you feel like crying, you'll let the tears come.

It seems crazy, but in a little while—sometimes just a minute or two—you'll realize you already feel better. You'll be clearer, calmer. Sometimes there's a moment of clarity, a new perspective about yourself or the situation. I usually write down any new awareness that comes, though after some missteps, I've learned to give myself time before making any decisions based on that changed perception. Whatever comes next, I'm less afraid. I've shown I can handle any emotion that arises.

Getting out of your head
to feel your feelings...*is healing.*

It's how you prove to yourself that your emotions matter. That YOU matter.

And that, my friends, is self-love.

26.

Honor Your Uniqueness
{Loving Wonderful, Weird Me}

There is a 'rightness' to loving ourselves, an instinctual tendency we're all born with. Watch any baby make faces in the mirror and you'll see what I mean. Really young children adore seeing pictures of themselves. They'll coo and laugh and marvel at the wonderful creation the universe has made. Deep down, they know they're special.

We all do—for a while.

Then something happens. Gradually and without our understanding, usually when we're still very young, we learn to conform to the ideas of our family, our peers, and our culture in order to be accepted. Maybe your ears had a unique shape, and to keep you from being teased, your mom changed your haircut to cover them. Or maybe you pronounced your R's differently and were sent to speech therapy.

These actions may have come from a place of love, but to our childish minds, the message was *How You Really Are Isn't Good.* So we changed. We hid. We deflected and pretended to be something we weren't.

Things got worse when we hit our teenage years and tried to attract romantic partners. Barraged by perfected images from our culture, we shined the harsh light of self-criticism on ourselves, hating every perceived blemish, turning ourselves into human pretzels in hopes that the right guy or girl would find us attractive. The message we internalized then was clear:

'Fit the Mold or You'll Be Alone Forever.'

Really?

{No wonder we tried so hard.}

Some managed to escape the conformity trap. Or, more to the point, they intentionally DIDN'T conform, thumbing their nose at any societal convention, even those that may have been genuinely good for them. Sometimes the rebellion was so extreme, they became clichés—the opposite of the uniqueness they wanted to achieve.

Most of us hit adulthood with a long set of rules for how we 'should' be and find ourselves falling short. Some rules contradict others, some are flat impossible for anyone to achieve and have any kind of satisfying life. It's no wonder we medicate ourselves into oblivion.

There's a better way, and that's to <u>love your weirdness</u>— while understanding that your weirdness is completely normal.

Here's an example from my own life. This may sound strange, but I hate condiments. You know, the ketchup and mustard sitting on the table at some restaurants? I think they're disgusting! I mean, who wants to squirt something onto their FOOD that's been sitting out at room temperature for God-knows-how-long, touched by everyone who's sat there in the last month.

Gross!!!!

Before learning to love myself, I was sort of embarrassed about this quirk. Other people don't seem to mind condiments, after all. And they're literally EVERYWHERE. *Maybe I'm the one who's weird*, I used to think.

Maybe I'm wrong.

And that's where loving yourself comes in. Now, instead of asking whether my quirk makes me wrong, I ask whether it hurts anyone including me. My condiment phobia was simple: hell no, it doesn't hurt anyone if I think condiments are gross— (because they ARE!)

Other characteristics haven't been so easy. I'm a forward-moving, big-picture kind of guy who hates getting bogged down with minutiae. There used to be some internal shame attached to this, because sometimes I had trouble getting projects to turn out the way I wanted. Now, rather than gripe at myself for not being good at detail work, I've learned to embrace my uniqueness and pay people to do what they're great at, while I focus on areas where I can shine.

It's like the adage about judging a fish for its ability to climb a tree.

What if, starting today, you stop apologizing for all those strange, annoying, odd, peculiar, and unusual qualities that make you, you? What if, instead, you say, "This is me! Wonderful, weird me. And these are my characteristics, some helpful, some maddening, and all mine. I'll take responsibility for any that hurt me or others by finding ways to work around them. And I'll love myself for every damn one!"

The essential lesson I've learned in life is to just be yourself. Treasure the magnificent being that you are and recognize first and foremost you're not here as a human being only. You're a spiritual being having a human experience.
~ Wayne Dyer

When you learn to embrace your weirdness instead of running from it, something unexpected and wonderful happens. You begin to appreciate others' funky characteristics, even those that used to make you mad. We'll talk about loving our shadow later, but the reality is that accepting ourselves—quirks and all—and loving ourselves completely is the only path toward loving others exactly as they are.

The one enduring truth in the universe is Love. When we direct it toward ourselves by celebrating our oddities, we begin to see ourselves and every other being as worthy of love. We feel love, share love, embody love. In every breath, every moment, every detail…we become love in human form.

And that's pretty weird…and wonderful!

27.

Learn to Say 'NO!'

No.

No, thanks.

Not this time.

Nuh-uh. Nope.

Not for me. Please take me off your list.

Absolutely not. Don't ask again...

No f*cking way.

How strong is your NO? Do you feel queasy reading those words and imagining yourself saying them? Do you find yourself wanting to apologize, explain, or justify? Do you sometimes wish people wouldn't ask so you don't have to disappoint them? Or do you squeak out a 'maybe,' hoping they'll forget and bother someone else?

Some of us are taught that saying 'no' makes us selfish. Mean people say no, nice people say *yes*. So, we adapt and adjust, wanting to do the right thing. Someone asks, you reluctantly say yes. Then you tweak your schedule and reshuffle your priorities, telling yourself things will slow down eventually.

Of course, it never does. People will always want things from you. And that's okay.

But if everyone else's priorities come first, you get worn down and resentful, wondering why your own needs always seem to come last. You find yourself staring wistfully at that unfinished novel as you grab your keys to dart out the door to help a friend for the fifth time this week.

Or maybe you're like me, less worried about making people unhappy as you are about missing out on a great opportunity. There are a million worthwhile projects out there and some of us love keeping our options open. Saying no closes doors, so even if we're pretty sure it's a no, we can't help feeling regret about what will never be.

But the truth is this:

Having a sure, clear 'no' generates incredible power behind your 'yes.'

Think of it this way. The energy you use to create your thoughts, actions, emotions, relationships, and words is your creative life force. I've come to believe we are all channels for this power, an energy that is limitless, wondrous, and available to all.

I believe that force is Love.

Now think about exactly where you want your creative force to flow. I suggest making a list of your priorities, such as career, spiritual development, physical health, creative projects, relationships with family, financial security, or service to others.

After you write down all the areas of your life that matter, put them in order of importance. Be honest. And don't judge the list or compare your list with anyone else's. If financial security is a huge need, that's fine. If saving the environment is your real passion, put it in the first position. My experience is that personal growth and spiritual development make all the other items flow more easily, but your list will be yours alone. Give yourself permission to let it evolve over time. Now test your list. If you only had a year to live, which would be the most important? What if there was only a month?

Once your priorities are noted and ranked, make a second column on your paper. In this column, write down how much time you spend every week on each activity, whether it's ten minutes or ten hours. Now compare the columns. Where do you spend the most time?

Do your time investments align with your priorities?

If you're like me the first time I did this exercise, some of my highest priorities received the least attention. If your priorities don't match up with how you invest your time, it's a good bet you struggle with saying no.

Remember that your YES gets its power from your NO.

So, how do you get better at saying NO?
Practice!

Try it now. Say 'no' silently in your head, then relax your shoulders and take a few deep breaths. Do it a few times. Now imagine someone you don't know very well asking you for a favor, and practice again by simply saying, "No." Play the mental game again, this time with something you're lukewarm about. Tell your imaginary favor-asker you'll let them know at a specific time later today. Then say no.

There's no such thing as maybe.

If it's not "Hell, yes," it's "Hell, *no!*"

Keep practicing, imagining closer relationships and people your genuinely care about. Now put a mark on your calendar and commit to saying no a dozen times a day—to telemarketers, coworkers, the person at the drive-through. Say it with a smile, use a kind voice, but make it a complete sentence. As you get better, try it out on friends and family. Be patient. Remember to breathe. I promise it gets easier.

In a week, you'll notice small changes. In two, you'll be more comfortable saying no. At the end of three weeks, I predict you'll feel a significant shift.

For some of us, the change is seismic. Your energy will flow where you want it, where it does the most good for you and those you care about.

Your no will be clear, kind, and free of resentment.

And your yes will be powered by that awesome, infinite, universal force called *Love.*

28.

Others Don't Need to Suffer for You to Feel Good

I really want to challenge you here, because you'll need some gut-level honesty if you want to absorb this lesson.

No-one likes to see others suffer...

...Or do they?

If we're honest, most of us admit we get a sense of satisfaction when some jerk finally gets what they deserve. Heck, whole movie franchises are built on good guys whupping up on the bad guys. (I'm looking at you, Diehard!) Now I want to invite you to grow beyond that impulse.

Because self-love means having compassion for all beings, at all times, in all circumstances.

And here's where it gets hard: that compassion needs to be unconditional.

Let me state that a different way, because it's super important. *The level of compassion we have for others always mirrors the internal feelings we have for ourselves. If we want to show love and compassion for others, we need to be completely loving and compassionate toward ourselves, and vice versa.*

Many of this book's principles are easy to embrace. This one may prick your ego. If so, that's okay. Try to be open if you can, especially since this isn't a new concept. One of the oldest prayers in Western religion asks God to forgive our trespasses AS we forgive those who've trespassed against us, and most spiritual philosophies revolve around some version of doing unto others as we'd have done to us.

So, here's the truth:

Feeling good seeing someone else suffer usually means, that at some unconscious level, you also believe you deserve to suffer.

But suffering (feeling shameful or unworthy) makes you feel cut off and alone. The little kid inside us can't stand being utterly alone, so he or she searches for someone else who is 'bad' too and is relieved to find them. "I may be worthless," he or she thinks, "But at least I'm not out here by myself."

What if you aren't bad, though? What if, despite your mistakes—even the serious ones—you're still completely worthy of love, even if you've been a total ass? What if your terrible action came out of an adaptation—or maladaptation—to a childhood wound you haven't yet faced? What if ALL humans' terrible actions result from adaptations to these wounds?

What if, when you screw up, you say to yourself, "Wow, that wasn't cool. You're going to have crappy consequences, and you'll need to do whatever you can to make this right, especially with those you've hurt. I'm really sorry you made this choice AND I LOVE YOU."

Don't we all deserve compassion, even as we face the natural consequences of our behavior?

Now, turn that compassion outward, toward every being. What would that look like? I like to imagine someone whose spiritual development I admire (say, the Dalai Lama, or Mother Teresa) confronting a hardened criminal facing a death sentence. There would be sadness, healing acceptance, even forgiveness. Someone whose life rests on the solid bedrock of loving themselves is able to view everyone, even those who behave horrifically, as worthy of compassion—

even when those people receive consequences for their actions. This isn't about making excuses. Bad decisions lead to bad consequences. It's totally appropriate to set boundaries, and some people are so dysfunctional they lose their right to freedom.

But everyone needs compassion, even in their worst moment.

Especially those who've harmed you—because having compassion for them in their worst moment gives you the freedom to love yourself in YOUR worst moment.

And that's what allows us to face our mistakes and grow.

Kicking our own asses never creates any lasting changes in our behavior. No one responds to being shamed (being told we're unlovable) even when the person doing the shaming is inside our own head. Beating ourselves up this way leaves us with three options: Fight, flight, or freeze. Faced with our internal hatred, we have no choice but to argue, escape, or numb out.

We can't face our failure, so we unconsciously look for someone else to carry our shame—and the cycle continues. Sometimes the cycles become lifelong patterns, repeated problems we never seem to overcome.

So, the next time you feel warm satisfaction at seeing some jerk get what he or she deserves, mind that impulse to find the place inside yourself where you feel less-than. Then, bring the feeling to the surface, uncover the event (or mistake) that led to the feeling, and find compassion for the wounded person who's responsible. If you're unflinching in your practice, you'll learn to forgive yourself (and others) for mistakes and instead choose different actions and responses. You'll find yourself growing out of old, unhelpful behaviors and letting go of self-destructive patterns.

Keep at it, and you'll reach a whole new level of peace, seeing everyone as worthwhile and valuable, no matter who they are. You won't be perfect, and you'll be totally okay with that, because you're now operating from a new level of maturity built on love.

You'll feel part of all that Is......And it's amazing!

29.

We're All Messed Up
{It's Just A Matter of Degrees}

All humans have issues. We're spiritual beings having a human experience, with unique histories that generate all sorts of adaptations and weird methods of coping. Depending on where we are in our current emotional development, we all fall somewhere on the spectrum between raw, selfish fear (ego) and pure unconditional love (spirit). The only question is where?

Take the opposing examples of a serial killer like Jeffrey Dahmer and spiritual leader Mahatma Gandhi. Obviously these two men followed very different life paths, with profoundly different results. Though he was noted for his peaceful manner, Gandhi was still human. He had fears, annoyances, quirks, and petty thoughts, same as everyone else. So why did Gandhi choose a path of service to humanity while Dahmer chose murder?

I believe the key difference lies in awareness, acceptance, and willingness to take personal responsibility.

As Michael Singer talks about in his book, THE UNTETHERED SOUL, our conscious mind can serenely observe our thoughts and emotions, or it can get drawn into the drama and lose all perspective. Every day we experience hundreds of thoughts, feelings, and events that literally come and go without a hitch. Then something grabs our emotional attention, we get disturbed, and our mind races to tell a story to justify our feeling. Maybe someone at work says something that pricks us, and we're offended. We remember all the times other people have hurt us. We're on the defensive, guarding our sore place. Within minutes, we're unhappy with life. Our job sucks, our coworkers are assholes, and we hate the carpet in our office.

Now, we've surrendered our inner peace without a fight.

What?

Anytime we lose perspective, ego takes over. Our mind tells us that other people, places, and things need to change so we'll feel good again. Maybe we blame ourselves, and resolve to be more powerful (fit, richer, tougher, more beautiful) so we won't feel the pain. We're caught up in the story, immersed in our internal drama. And we believe it's all true.

Without awareness, ego can drive the train for a very long time, especially if we don't love ourselves enough to look for a better way.

Awareness offers freedom.

Observing ourselves with gentle curiosity allows us to notice our reactions without being captivated by the story. When we find ourselves angry, justifying, or defending, we can stop and return to our quiet center of simply watching without judgment. We become present in the moment, able to make choices without unconsciously sabotaging ourselves.

To make good choices, we need acceptance.

No matter how I feel about it, things ARE as they ARE. Every day we all experience inconveniences, challenges, and injustices, large and small, and we're able to accept most of them without a second thought.

But some things grab me. I'm able to pay an ATM fee with no problem yet get seriously pissed when a restaurant adds an automatic gratuity to my check. Both require acceptance if I want to maintain inner peace. Acceptance means acknowledging the event and noticing my response without trying to change either one. Sometimes it isn't easy. I breathe, relax my chest and shoulders, and name whatever feeling I'm having without generating a story to defend it. If I'm resisting the feeling, I notice that too.

Think of it as watching a sports event from up in the booth rather than being on the field. It's a way to gain perspective. Once I've noticed my reaction and named my feeling, it's time to do the hardest part.

Take responsibility for my reaction.

Going back to the idea that people, places, and events ARE what they ARE, and remembering that we deal with thousands of unfair, inconvenient, and challenging things each day that don't even register, we come to this truth:

151

Anything that disturbs our emotional equilibrium is our own internal stuff being triggered.

Let me say that again, because this is the real difference-maker on where we fall on the spectrum between ego and spirit. When I have a strong reaction that takes me out of the present moment, there's a place inside me that requires healing. And the only one who can do that work is me.

So, I ask myself what inner wound needs my attention? Which deep-seated insecurity am I trying to protect? What pain am I avoiding?

And the big one: How can I let that pain come to the surface and then release it?

The wound may be from long ago. Most of them are. But your reaction is coloring your reality right now, clouding your ability to make decisions from a place of internal calm, from love instead of ego. It's your trigger, your wound, your reaction…and therefore your responsibility.

Everyone struggles sometimes. But it gets easier with practice. And the result of seeing ourselves moving higher (however slowly) on the spectrum between ego and love is that we're able to recognize when someone else is responding to their triggers. We're able to see our fellow messed-up humans as wounded people with a lot to learn, just like us. We stop taking their reactions personally, because we know they are responsible for healing their triggers, same as us. Awareness, acceptance, responsibility.

Some days we'll do pretty well, others not so much. Either way, we all deserve compassion. Because we're all messed up, it's just a matter of degrees.

30.

When Things Go Wrong, Shift to Love

Love is the antidote to everything.

Love means something different to everyone. So you understand how we're using love in this chapter, in this context, we're looking at Love vs. Fear.

Biologically, our brains are wired for fear. It's the way we used to survive, literally, by looking for the next shoe—or next spear—to drop. The reptilian brain includes the brainstem and the cerebellum, which are reliable but tend to be somewhat rigid and compulsive, hence the name 'reptilian.' Now, in modern times, without the daily fear of death, our brains transfer that 'fear scanning' to less deadly things, like money woes, or if that next latte will be hot enough, or how bad the traffic will be. *Awful stuff!*

Fear is only useful when making life or death decisions in the moment.

After that, the Law of Diminishing Returns takes over. In short order, fear is not serving you at ALL! In fact, it's hurting you. That's the time to shift to love.

When real tragedy strikes, that's another issue altogether. A death. An accident. A large loss of some kind. I'm not saying ignore the feelings that come up, I'm saying think of something that represents love—a person, a thing, or a memory—and hold that image in your head to help *replace* the fear and awful feelings. It's good to feel your feelings (good or not so good). It is through our feelings that we know what direction to head. When you are at an uncomfortable fork in the road, the best course is choosing love; especially when things don't feel good.

Slowly, and over time, you will learn how to use those good thoughts more effectively.

It takes an intentional human to shift to love.

You can do it! When the trigger appears, that is opportunity knocking on your spiritual door. Are you going to answer it with LOVE? Or Fear? Ask yourself, what would LOVE do in this moment? And if *I* represent love, what would love do?

Emotionally, love is the antidote and cancels out fear so it takes the electric charge out of that 'fight or flight' knee-jerk reaction our reptilian brains have, and therefore facilitates inner-peace. And, the outcome will probably be better. Whatever decision-making processes you need to go through will be more measured, calm, and logical if you can get away from the bad emotional reaction.

Without fear, or ego involved, things become more manageable; more approachable.

Ask yourself, what am I gaining by emotional hand-wringing, holding onto fear, anguish, or anxiety? Why am I letting THAT take up valuable real estate in my head? Allow love to take its place. Let go of the inner censor. Stick a toe into the world of love and see how it feels.

Think of love as that eternal and infinite compass that resides in you. It's that place within that tells you who you are, what is best for you, and shows you the way to healthier and better choices. When you tap into it, you tap into the universal flow.

We are all creators.
It's time to design and
construct a new choice.

Every journey starts with awareness. <u>A</u>wareness transforms into <u>BE</u>coming. Point A to Point B is a line that only you can draw. How will you travel it? I hope with a new awareness of **love** and its powerful transformative properties.

"True life is lived when tiny changes occur."
LEO TOLSTOY

Practice. Practice. Practice. Create space for yourself to do just that. Silence the Critic and just feel. Emotions are the key to your destiny. They fuel your life and drive your choices. So, practice shifting to the universal and healing emotion of **love**. Fear will pass more quickly, like a cold breeze. Then, the sun will find you and you can embrace the rays. Like the sun, love will warm you and radiate out to others. Once you shift to love, you will feel like you've captured lightening in a bottle...and you *have!*

What the Heck is Self-Love Anyway?

Final Thoughts...

"There is a candle in your heart, ready to be kindled.
There is a void in your soul, ready to be filled.
You feel it, don't you?" ~ Mawlana Jalal-al-Din Rumi

There are some who believe self-love is merely looking into a mirror, gazing into one's eyes and repeating the phrase: "I love you" over and over again until you feel a change. While you might feel a slight shift, how is this really going to work long term?

Well, my friends, I believe there's more to it and I hope you've gleaned something eye-opening and heart-opening from these pages, because—as I have learned—the simple (yet challenging) concept of self-love is the keystone to all other learning and growth.

Once you decide to metabolize self-love into your life, it will super-charge all other self-growth, spiritual exploration, and self-help. When you become aware (and responsible) for your thoughts, feelings, and actions, you begin to feel that life is working <u>for</u> you, not against you. The world around you opens up; becomes more friendly. Your future widens and former ideas you thought improbable, suddenly become possible.

I'm sharing this with you because, as I connect the dots backwards over my life, I too have been through dark times. My darkest days began in 2005 when I turned 40 and suddenly lost my 13-year marriage, my quarter-million-dollar job, and the market crashed leaving me nearly broke. I began to wonder at night whether I wanted to wake up in the morning.

I thought I was living in 'hell' but it birthed my personal development, self-help and spiritual journey, unaware of the lifeline it would be later. The road was rocky. Many times, I fell into the quicksand of depression and despair. But, I still heard the voice of Walt Disney floating in my head: *"Keep moving forward..."* So, that's what I did and I began a daily self-care practice which ended up preparing me for the deeper lesson I was about to experience.

Now here's the thing, I ALWAYS thought the loss of a child would be the most devastating thing that could happen in the life of a parent... especially my own. Many nights, I went to bed worried that this was a possibility. I began to live in fear, anger, and resentment because I loved my boys unconditionally. *That's right!* In many ways I <u>hated</u> being a parent because unconditional love leaves you vulnerable. The fact is, I thought I would be so devasted—completely paralyzed for life—if something happened to one (or both) of my children. This was my story up until about a year before he passed. In fact, shortly after Connor's 18th birthday, I chose to give up worry, and allowed him his own path while I choose a daily practice of self-love.

My experience after my son's death ended up being the furthest thing from what I thought would happen. I had imagined "grief"—beyond painful grief—but that didn't happen to me.

Now don't get me wrong, losing Connor hurts and I miss him dearly. There are some days (in the year since he passed) when I feel very sad and yet it hasn't taken me down the road of no return. It didn't devastate my life like I thought it would.

There are as many ways to grieve as there are people—many paths and 'many roads to Rome,' if you will. None of them should be lessened or discounted as each of us has our own way to grieve. However, I grieved (and still do) with a blanket of love. This is what I call: Grieving with Love.

After finishing the first draft of this book, I began asking myself: *how has this happened? How* have I been relatively calm and able to grieve this way? Why didn't I go off the deep end? The answer, I believe, is <u>Self-Love</u>. My daily personal development, self-help and spiritual practice (and I don't mean religious) felt like a vaccination to the impending chaos; both small and large. The power of Self-Love (for me) created inner peace …even as the worse thing I could have imagined was happening in my life.

The countless self-help books I'd read—from the Inner Child Workshop (Hoffman), to the Heart Awakening Seminars (Insight), to the hundreds of YouTube video's, to hours of psychotherapy and a daily study group in *A Course In Miracles*—left me with a self-created blanket of love. <u>Self-Love.</u>

As I said in the beginning of the book; like the flight attendant who announces; 'If you're traveling with small children, place the oxygen mask on yourself *first*,…' I had chosen to do just that before he transitioned. Now I SEE why this was my journey.

While I can only speak of my own journey to self-discovery, there are many of you who have experienced deep trauma and feel as if you are in a 'living hell' right now. Some of you might be experiencing self-sabotaging behavior, drowning in limiting beliefs, trapped in a cycle of victimhood (or actually be one) or have deep-seated fears about life in general. This is when I ask you to reflect inward and seek professional or medical help.

Part of my journey included psychotherapy and working with trained professionals because, for a longest time, many things would trigger me and send me into a tailspin. By choosing people much wiser than me for help, it allowed me to piece together this puzzle of Self-Love and gave me a greater awareness of this thing called LIFE.

If you can relate to any of this and you feel like your life isn't working for you—perhaps you're struggling with health, divorce, the loss of a career or dear relationship—please seek out trained support. Hopefully the words in this book is a wakeup call to choosing a better way to live... a life of Self-Love. In the pages ahead, you'll find recommended readings to assist you on your own personal journey of discovery.

Now that we are at the end of the book, my invitation to you is to make a commitment to yourself to choose YOU every day and in every way, because life will reveal many answers over time on your journey to joy, fulfillment and inner peace. How you approach your journey may change in the weeks, months, and years ahead and my hope is that you make personal development, self-help, and/or spirituality a daily practice.

Thank you for reading and I've enjoyed moving through this process with you.

In Honor of...

Connor "Salty" Aslay
1999 - 2018

What the Heck is Self-Love Anyway?

Recommended Readings, Studies, Teachers, and Workshops

The following sample of my favorite readings, studies, teachers, and workshops have been the foundation of my personal growth, spiritual path, and self-help practice in the order I was introduced to each beginning in 1989.

You Can Heal Your Life ~ by Louise Hay

Creative Visualization ~ by Shakti Gawain

The Movie: *The Secret*

The Movie: *What The Bleep*

A Return To Love ~ by Marianne Williamson

The Four Agreements ~ by Don Miguel Ruiz

Unleash the Power Within Workshop ~ by Tony Robbins

The Untethered Soul ~ by Michael Singer

Wayne Dyer (Author) Video's on YouTube

Abraham Hicks (Esther & Jerry Hicks):
https://www.abraham-hicks.com/

The Karpman Drama Triangle

Mankind Project: The New Warrior Training Weekend
https://mankindproject.org/new-warrior-training-adventure/

Reverend Michael Bernard Beckwith: https://agapelive.com/

The Hoffman Process: https://www.hoffmaninstitute.org/

Insight Seminars Worldwide:
https://www.insightseminars.org/

A Course in Miracles by the Foundation For Inner Peace

As you can see, my journey to self-love has spanned 20 years, and in some ways, even after all this work, there are times when I feel I've only scratched the surface to deeper awareness. By the time you pick up this book, I'm sure there are many more roads I will have taken on this path of Self-Discovery.

As I've heard it said over and over again: Life is a Journey, Not a Destination. May your journey be filled with joy, fulfillment and inner peace.

About
the
Author

Known as America's Leading Midlife Dating & Relationship Coach, Jonathon Aslay is a defender and protector of women's hearts around the world. He helps women transform from attracting Mr. Wrong into finding their Mr. Right.

Jonathon, a successful entrepreneur, coach, speaker, and author of *Understand Men Now; The Relationships Men Commit To and Why.* Jonathon is like A GUY SPY to the male mind who truly understands the way a single or divorced man thinks and acts. He's a master at helping women recognize and distinguish the difference between men who are emotionally unavailable from those who are truly ready for love.

What the Heck is Self-Love Anyway?

Made in the USA
Columbia, SC
27 November 2022

72135737R00102